NO CAMPUS
FOR
WHITE MEN

NO CAMPUS FOR
FOR
WHITE MEN

THE TRANSFORMATION OF
HIGHER EDUCATION INTO
HATEFUL INDOCTRINATION

SCOTT GREER

WND BOOKS

NO CAMPUS FOR WHITE MEN

Published by WND Books, Washington, D.C. WND Books is a registered trademark of WorldNetDaily.com, Inc. ("WND")

Book designed by Mark Karis

WND Books are available at special discounts for bulk purchases. WND Books also publishes books in electronic formats. For more information call (541) 474-1776, e-mail orders@wndbooks.com, or visit www.wndbooks.com.

Paperback ISBN: 978-1-944229-62-7
eBook ISBN: 978-1-944229-63-4

Library of Congress Cataloging-in-Publication Data

Names: Greer, Scott, 1990-
Title: No campus for white men : the transformation of higher education into hateful indoctrination / Scott Greer ; foreword by Milo Yiannopoulos.
Description: Washington, D.C. : WND Books, 2017. | Includes bibliographical references and index.
Identifiers: LCCN 2016044833 (print) | LCCN 2016046657 (ebook) | ISBN 9781944229627 (hardcover) | ISBN 9781944229634 (e-book)
Subjects: LCSH: Education, Higher--United States. | Racism--United States. | College students--United States--Political activity.
Classification: LCC LA227.4 .G74 2017 (print) | LCC LA227.4 (ebook) | DDC 378.73--dc23
LC record available at https://lccn.loc.gov/2016044833

Printed in the United States of America
17 18 19 20 21 LBM 9 8 7 6 5 4 3 2

CONTENTS

FOREWORD

've had the grim pleasure in witnessing just how far American universities have devolved by speaking at many of them as part of my tastefully named and by no means offensive Dangerous Faggot tour.

Scott Greer illustrates my controversial tour stop at DePaul University as part of his new book, *No Campus for White Men*, but I'd like to share another aspect of the story that I myself only learned after the event—it illustrates exactly what we are up against on campuses today.

I had my hands full on stage. A male protester, perhaps the only one amongst the group, was blowing a whistle into the stage microphone to create a deafening cacophony, shouting deranged slogans at the audience, and threatening to punch my lights out. A female accomplice with the horrific fashion sense to wear a fanny pack in public was alternatively dancing, mumbling to anyone close by, and shaking her finger in my face.

As Scott points out in the book, school administrators and police stood by passively taking in the spectacle. That was the first clue that they condoned the actions of the Black Lives Matter hooligans intent on shutting down my speech.

Another bit of drama was related to me by one of my closest associates, who had a front-row seat to the insanity of the DePaul administration. The main body of protesters was comprised of black women who sat down at the foot of the stage and linked arms. I guess their goal was to block the police or university officials from walking up to the stage, but they needn't have bothered, the authorities were on their side.

One DePaul administrator in particular, a big oaf of a man in a purple shirt, was constantly pacing in front of this protest line. None of his attention was spent on the protestors, however, he was focusing on the crowd, which was growing upset and chanting for the protesters to be removed so the event could carry on.

When a young doughy white woman left her seat and approached the picket line, the purple-shirted man leapt into action. He stood in her way with arms raised and said something to the effect of "No, no, no, you can't come up here!" She petulantly replied "I'm with these sisters!" and he immediately got out of her way with a speed and grace one would think impossible for his imposing bulk. An extra large hole was made for the hefty young lady, and she locked arms with Black Lives Matter to prevent free speech at DePaul.

The key part of this story is the administrator's reaction when he learned the student wasn't arguing against the protest, but rather joining it. It left me wondering what the hell was going on that DePaul would try to stop legitimate attendees of an event, but not protesters disrupting a speech.

The primary reason I share this story is that the entire incident galvanized me to raise the bar for the second leg of the Dangerous Faggot tour. We rented a bus and plastered my face on the side, and created elaborate visual presentations for every tour stop in the second half of 2016.

All of the delicate snowflakes triggered by the Dangerous Faggot tour can thank the DePaul Black Lives Matter children for raising my tour to new heights.

And triggered they are—consider the hypersensitivity of the students at the University of Pittsburgh. Following my speech, the student government convened a meeting for students to "understand the hurt and pain" that my speech caused. "I felt I was in danger, and I felt so many people in that room were in danger," one student moaned before demanding the university provide counselors for those who were "traumatized." The student body president reportedly "teared up" after "hearing students' experiences as a result of Milo Yiannopoulos."

There is no question the campus crybabies, popularly known as social justice warriors, look like fools to the general public. Even the *Daily Show* is making fun of them now. In a typically unfunny skit called "Outrage Court: Trigger Warnings" they opined:

College kids should grow a pair. If our kids grow up thinking the world is safe spaces and trigger warnings, then, hell, how are we going to protect ourselves from Russia? Hell, how are we going to stand up to Jamaica? All they do is come in here triggering us with their damn reggae and their ganja and their jerk chicken.

It is painfully clear that many schools are coddling students, more concerned with their feelings than the growth of their intellect. But the Left does not care about the feelings of the conservative students who sponsor me to speak and are consequently subjected to social ridicule and even physical threats. Nor do they care about the safety of the Duke Lacrosse team or fraternity members at the University of Virginia who faced death threats and had their house vandalized to make cheap political points.

This is where Scott Greer's excellent book, *No Campus for White Men,* shines a light on the real issues on campus. The problem is not just overgrown crybabies and helicopter parenting, but an extreme version of identity politics, which encourages students to demand power and privilege on the sole basis of their race, gender, or sexual orientation. The flipside is that they want to disenfranchise and humiliate everyone who is not part of their designated victim groups—especially straight, white men. Greer traces this theme back to the cultural Marxist Frankfurt School theoretician Herbert Marcuse's call for "repressive tolerance," according to which the views of the majority must be stamped out so that revolutionary minorities can take power.

The arguments in *No Campus for White Men* will not sit well with liberal critics of campus culture like Bill Maher. They understand that blue-haired feminists screaming over a difference of opinion makes the Left look bad but will never be willing to confront the underlying premises of victim culture. In fact, they agree with it—they just want to seem snarky and intelligent instead of insane when they make their demands.

Many conservatives do not want to address these problems as well. As usual, the cowardly "cuckservatives" desperately want to avoid any discussion of race or gender. But it's also comforting for baby boomer and geriatric *National Review* subscribers to scoff at those damn kids instead of actually confronting the ideology that their generations created.

Don't get me wrong, we still need to make fun of the blue-haired feminists and SJWs. Crazy, obese protesters will always have a special place in my heart. But if we are going to defeat the Left—both on campus, and in America at large—we need to understand their goals and motivations. *No Campus for White Men* is the first book to truly do so.

America has a long way to go to return universities to their rightful places as centers of learning, free speech, and controversial ideas. Scott Greer's *No Campus for White Men* is a good step in this battle, and I am proud to consider him a compatriot in the battle for America's higher education.

—MILO YIANNOPOULOS, MILWAUKEE, WISCONSIN, DECEMBER 2016

INTRODUCTION

American universities were once the cultivators of the nation's brightest minds, the gateway to the middle class, and forums for the exchange of ideas and innovations.

Now they can't tolerate chalk marks in support of a certain Republican presidential candidate.

In March 2016, students at Emory University found themselves the victims of "chalkings" proclaiming the oh-so horrifying slogan "Trump 2016." This unbearable sight caused some at the Atlanta-based school to fret for their safety and condemn the chalky political speech as a form of racial intimidation. Because these students felt so threatened by fairly tame political speech, they demanded their university president condemn the act in the strongest terms possible.

Emory's president initially said he would not condemn the chalking because it wasn't his place to pass judgment on electoral politics. After an intense, hour-long meeting with irate activists, the administrator changed his tune and issued a mealy-mouthed statement sympathizing with the aggrieved and promising new measures to ensure more "social justice opportunities."

Emory's student government association showed less restraint, denouncing the monstrous chalk markings as representing "particularly bigoted opinions, policies and rhetoric directed at populations represented at Emory University." The body further expressed "sympathy for the pain experienced by members of our community" and released emergency funds to provide counseling sessions for those emotionally scarred by the chalk.

According to one university official, there was so much outrage at the harmless chalk marks because students from "marginalized groups" experience unimaginable levels of intolerance, and they get very upset at any signs of possible injustice. These protected classes of students have every right to demand a campus free from offense.[1]

Sadly, Emory was not alone in witnessing student hysteria over pro-Trump chalkings. Students at the University of Michigan called the cops upon seeing chalk marks in support of Trump at their campus. One incensed student even demanded a special hotline to report any future cases of offensive markings.[2]

In response to the hysteria at Emory, students from across

the country participated in a social media campaign dubbed #TheChalkening, which encouraged individuals to chalk pro-Trump messages at their respective campuses as an act of protest against campus political correctness. Students at more than a hundred campuses participated in the endeavor, and it became a trending topic on Twitter in early April 2016.

One newly elected student representative at the University of Tennessee at Chattanooga was particularly proud of her chalking and tweeted it out with the caveat that half of her campus may hate it. And many of that young student's peers did indeed hate it. A few hours after tweeting the image, the SGA coalition of which she was a part demanded she resign over showing support for Donald Trump. That call was issued in order to calm the growing fury of UTC's black community, which found the chalking an endorsement of bigotry.[3]

The wave of outrage over Trump chalkings continued to spiral throughout the spring of 2016. Ohio University canceled its Greek Week and imposed diversity lessons as a punishment against its fraternity and sorority system. The reason for this action? A few fraternity members drew a Trump wall on a campus structure specifically designed for student illustrations.[4] At Tulane University football players destroyed a sandbag wall bearing the Trump name, erected on a fraternity's private property. No punitive action was taken against the vandals.[5] DePaul University banned all political chalk messages in response to a claim from its Black Student Union that a pro-Trump chalking constituted a "hate crime."[6]

The hysteria over pro-Trump chalkings is just one particularly egregious example of the kind of politically correct insanity currently embroiling American higher education. "Safe spaces" are erected to protect students from the dangerous ideas of conservative speakers. Presidents hand in resignations over accusations of facilitating "systemic racism." Stifling speech codes punish predominantly conservative opinions while leaving far-left viewpoints unmolested.

The most notorious examples of campus insanity occurred in November 2015 when two major universities became enmeshed in campus-wide protests. Yale University witnessed mass demonstrations over a professor chiding students for being upset over Halloween costume "cultural appropriation" and a false claim of fraternity racism. The University of Missouri saw its system president ignominiously resign over a poop swastika and other unverified claims of discrimination. Mizzou student activists went into full-blown hysteria over the ruckus, with threatened journalists trying to cover their protests, and even went as far as to erroneously claim the Ku Klux Klan had risen from the dead to invade their campus.[7]

Colleges have been breeding grounds for radicalism for quite some time. It's not that shocking for students to take up causes that seem loony to the rest of America. Exhibit A: the turbulence of the 1960s and early '70s that plagued higher education.

But there are major differences between the campus radicalism of today and the protests of the past.

For one, students in the 1960s demanded more freedom, particularly freedom of speech. Today's students demand less freedom (the majority anyway) and wish to infringe on the freedom of speech.

What happened?

It is a common refrain to suggest that today's students want to curtail free speech because they are overgrown crybabies incapable of hearing out different viewpoints. Personalities from all political persuasions and stations in life have echoed this opinion. Former New York mayor Michael Bloomberg,[8] comedian Bill Maher,[9] the University of Chicago,[10] every conservative commentator you can think of, and even President Barack Obama[11] have all chastised young students for failing to listen to different points of view. Reasons for that have, likewise, ranged all over the place. The consensus is that kids are just too darn pampered these days and have receded into prolonged infantilism.

That mentality was encapsulated in a popular column by conservative law professor Glenn Reynolds that demanded raising the voting age to twenty-five in response to recent campus turmoil.[12] If the majority of college students can no longer participate in political discussions—as evidenced by protests at the University of Missouri—then they should wait until they graduate and experience the real world before being allowed into a polling station.

While it may seem fitting to disenfranchise those who wish to shut down all forms of speech that offend them, the stereotype of the perpetually offended and censorious college student does not apply to all millennials. Not even the majority of them.

What we are presently witnessing at college campuses is not the result of overtly coddled backgrounds and helicopter parenting. It's the beginning of an extreme version of identity politics. An identity politics that encourages students to demand power and privilege on the sole basis of their race, gender, or sexual orientation. An identity politics that hopes to disenfranchise and humiliate large segments of one's fellow students. An identity politics that's increasingly bordering on outright hatred for white people, especially white men.

The marauding activists who charged into a Dartmouth University library in late 2015 to make everyone proclaim that black lives matter and to physically assault white library denizens who showed insufficient enthusiasm for the endeavor upheld this ugly political style. Naturally, their victims were also berated with antiwhite language.[13] This is a textbook example of racialism taking over higher education.

The insanity is the work of a very vocal and very powerful minority of students—a coalition of the aggrieved—who push these extreme identity politics. Some within this coalition are committed leftists eager to embrace the latest social justice trend. Most fall into one of the identities that give a young adult privileges and moral sway at a college campus. From African-American activists demanding dramatic expansions of racial quotas to transsexuals urging the elimination of gender-specific pronouns, a protected class is nearly always at the center of a college outrage.

Just take a look at how mere chalkings of Donald Trump's name have triggered pandemonium and official sympathy with the offended. Administrators were willing to believe these stories of racial intimidation because they teach that our society is infected with unconscious bigotry. They will not challenge a fundamental belief of campus orthodoxy to defend harmless political speech. If protected classes feel threatened and/or offended, then school officials are helpless to say otherwise. That's why claims of offense are taken so seriously. It's why efforts at transforming campuses into large-scale safe spaces—no matter how impossible or unconstitutional—are even attempted.

By facilitating this form of identity politics, America's college campuses serve as a disturbing preview of the possible social and political discourse of America's future. The kids marching today to shut down a speaker they don't like could very well be the senators, judges, and newspaper editors of tomorrow. Our country could be run by people who think extreme identity politics is grand and we should strive to ensure these protected classes are never offended again. And it all could begin with colleges doling out spoils to those with the highest degree of victim status.

What an awful precedent for the rest of American society.

Higher education now incentivizes students to adopt and exploit an identity that can give them a leg up in the Victimhood Olympics. This, in turn, encourages the "victimized" students to hate their fellow classmates who are assigned the oppressor identity by the mandated form of campus politics. Additionally, it leads these grievance mongers to also hate traditional America and Western civilization.

If they're taught to see themselves as oppressed by all the great institutions of the West, why would these activists come to love the achievements of the nation and civilization in which they reside?

With all that hatred built up, student activists are making a bid to take control over higher education under the guise of victimhood signaling. Current campus politics is a struggle for power, and the Left wants to assign it based on race, gender, and sexual orientation.

No Campus for White Men aims to uncover what has led our once-prized institutions of learning to become incubators for this extreme type of identity politics. For years colleges have pursued policies that favor students based on their race, gender, and sexual orientation. Affirmative action has become a cornerstone in higher education, with bitter consequences. Colleges encourage students to adopt a special identity because of a spoils system that rewards students based on who they claim to be, not on what they have accomplished. Both as an inevitable result and in defense of affirmative action, ideologies have arisen on campus that go much further than rectifying past injustices.

Diversity is pedestaled as a magical attribute that makes everyone smarter and more loving—contrary to all evidence. A new system for awarding status that is no longer based on rights or honor, but on victimhood, has been erected at colleges. Political correctness, of course, is enshrined and made more pernicious in hunting down the tiniest of slights, known as *microaggressions*. The behavior and culture of white folks is pathologized into categories such as "white privilege"—motivating those with low melanin counts to seek redemption by bending the knee before protected classes.

Multiple and sometimes competing identities abound on college campuses. Protesters expressing support for Black Lives Matter are advocating racial activism in that they believe jobs, scholarship, and subsidies should be awarded to a person solely on the basis of his or her race. Feminists shrieking about rape culture wish to impose an institutional double standard when it comes to gender relations. Transgender students hoping to eradicate biological categories demand everyone to be addressed by pronouns straight out of a science fiction film. All are expressions of the kind of malicious identity politics that now dominate university life.

The one group not allowed to have a powerful identity is whites. Every identity bases itself on opposition to either "whiteness" or the majority culture, or both. No form of "white identity" would be allowed by either administrators or activists. Individuals who join with the activists who can't claim protected class status are given short shrift by their supposed allies. Those students, particularly Greek life participants, who don't join in the social justice cause are singled out for harassment.

Thanks to speech codes that privilege liberal views and silence dissenting ones, social justice warriors are at an advantage in trying to punish their foes—both fellow students and wayward professors. This is to say nothing of the effect it has on freedom of speech at places that are supposed to serve as marketplaces for ideas. While campus activists may enjoy the backing of administrators, some have pushed their luck in promoting hoaxes to achieve their goals. As long as it fits an established narrative, the deceit typically goes unnoticed until it's exposed by further investigation.

All of these factors combine to make higher education toxic for serious intellectual development and bode ill for the country's future. If everyone is vying to be the top victim and the most oppressed by Western civilization, campus life becomes more likely to descend into a veritable war of all against all. College is already becoming a major financial burden for young adults. Coupled with diminishing job prospects, campus insanity makes a university education lose its traditional value. Colleges notorious for left-wing activism are already seeing enrollment drop to historic lows.[14]

The roots of these harmful developments can be found in our greater society, with all its polarization and obsession with minority victimhood. Colleges are places where these insidious elements can thrive and infect the minds of tomorrow's leaders. The values imparted during college will influence how those budding leaders manage our country in the years to come. The counterculture that arose in the 1960s led to the social transformations in the latter part of the twentieth century. The very same thing can happen with our current campus upheaval, with it serving as a forecast of America's future:

racial identity trumping all other forms of identity, with white identity the only kind not welcome in polite society

race resentment codified as a fact of life

everyone trying to claim victimhood to earn goodies from the state

free speech forsaken in favor of protecting the precious feelings of victim classes

authorities letting the privileged castes get away with nearly everything but zealously persecuting dissidents who challenge prevailing dogmas.

But hope for higher education isn't completely lost, and our institutions can still be returned to their original mission of enlightening young minds if people recognize the issue in time. If contemporary college culture isn't changed soon, America will have far more problems on its hands than coeds wailing over chalk marks.

1

CULT OF DIVERSITY

Colleges have changed dramatically from the quiet institutions they were once intended to be.

Arguably, the most decisive factor for the transformation of higher education is affirmative action.

In the United States, affirmative action is the umbrella term for the favorable policies—primarily in relation to employment and education policies—designed to benefit minority groups who claim to have suffered past discrimination.

Coming to the fore in the civil rights era, this policy

prescription was originally intended to diminish the inequalities caused by the country's legitimate cases of institutional racism. The term was popularized by President John F. Kennedy in his 1961 executive order establishing the Committee on Equal Employment Opportunity to eliminate hiring bias among government contractors. "The contractor will take affirmative action to ensure that applicants are employed, and that employees are treated during employment, without regard to their race, creed, color, or national origin," Kennedy's order read.[1]

The main argument for mandating affirmative action was the belief Jim Crow's effects were not going to disappear overnight. "You do not take a person who, for years, has been hobbled by chains and liberate him, bring him up to the starting line of a race and then say you are free to compete with all the others, and still just believe that you have been completely fair," President Lyndon B. Johnson said in justification of affirmative action in 1965.[2]

The federal government under these two administrations mandated that employers and various institutions commit themselves to ensuring previously disenfranchised minorities have equal access to jobs, education, and other opportunities. It's a policy that has so far gone unchallenged by any following presidential administration.

The minority group that was the intended beneficiary of these policies were African-Americans. Affirmative action aimed to give blacks, restricted at the voting booth and in the employment line, a compensatory leg up in American society. Due to the unique injustices done to them in the past, so-called positive discrimination was designed specifically to give African-Americans certain advantages in order for them to better integrate with mainstream society.

Since these policies first became law during the 1960s, white institutional racism has disappeared from our society. Black Americans now have every opportunity that white Americans have long enjoyed. Yet affirmative action is more firmly entrenched in our society than ever before. Once intended solely for African-Americans, myriad minorities are now eligible for its benefits. In Johnson's 1965 order, women were added to those who needed equal hiring mandates. Soon, the list grew to include American Indians, Hispanics, and even gays.[3]

The primary place where Americans will come in contact with this practice is the college admissions process. It is demonstrably clear that African-Americans, Hispanics, and a few other groups receive preferential treatment when it comes to earning admission into a university. Whites aren't so lucky and, increasingly, neither are Asians.

A study conducted by UCLA law professor Richard Sander found that most schools in states where racial preferences are allowed give blacks a more than five-to-one advantage over whites in the admissions process. This discrepancy is not primarily a result of superior academic performance on the part of African-American students. At the University of North Carolina–Chapel Hill, another study found black applicants scoring in the second-highest academic index category were accepted at a 100 percent rate for the year 2006. Whites and Asians in that same category registered only a 42 percent and 43 percent acceptance rate, respectively.[4]

Caucasians sometimes claim Native American ancestry in order to boost their chances in gaining entry to the upper echelons of higher education.[5] For example, Massachusetts senator and progressive heartthrob Elizabeth Warren allegedly checked the

Native American box when applying for a professorial position at Harvard Law School. Her blonde hair and lack of elite law school degree, interestingly, proved no obstacle to getting the job.[6]

Another prominent case of an applicant claiming a different race to get a spot in college is the brother of Indian American actress Mindy Kaling. Vijay Chokal-Ingam claimed to be a black man in his medical school applications to compensate for his middling grades and so-so MCAT test score. Chokal-Ingam went so far as to change his appearance by shaving his head and trimming his eyebrows and made sure to emphasize his middle name, JoJo, in the admissions process. The deception apparently worked as several top medical schools recruited the aspiring doctor in spite of his lackluster résumé.[7]

With this seeming bias toward certain minorities at the expense of other groups, it's easy to see how university admissions policies are challenged in court on the grounds of installing a new kind of discrimination. However, college administrators, judges, and other powerful figures still cling to affirmative action in the face of the haunting specter of reverse racism. The reasons for keeping it around include allegations that the effects of institutional racism still exist in "post-racial America" and that diversity offers *incredible* benefits to young students.

That institutional racism is still prevalent in our society has become a common view among the Left. Black Lives Matter activists shout it from the street corners, and Democratic politicians repeat it from the rally stage. The perception that whites are the unfair recipients of America's privileges lingers on in leftists' minds, and one way to combat this supposed discrepancy is through positive discrimination in college admissions. Even though the Supreme Court has explicitly ruled that racial quotas are unconstitutional, many campus activists demand them to rectify racial injustice. But these wayward minds should be forgiven for demanding an illegal item—college racial preferences basically constitute quotas in all but name. So it makes sense that they would call for them to be expanded to specifically require that a college have X number of students and faculty of a particular race.

The more popular argument for refuting opponents of affirmative action relies on just reiterating how great diversity is. In multiple Supreme Court cases, judges upheld minority preferences in admissions practices due to the belief that racial diversity is essential to higher education. This belief is based on the notion that being surrounded by people who differ from you in racial identity makes you smarter and better prepared for the world.

Interacting with people who differ from you in experiences and background obviously presents a great opportunity for expanding the horizons of young minds. But the kind of diversity envisioned by college administrators doesn't necessarily broaden minds—it's more about creating the conditions for group conflict and anti-majority sentiment. Students are encouraged in their application to indicate that they are non-white in order to gain entry. That reward on the application extends to the students' time at college and encourages them to pedestal their racial or other identity that got them into college in the first place. This diversity doesn't mean students with different political viewpoints or hailing from different income brackets interact with one another at the same tony campus. All it means is that colleges strive to achieve unwritten racial quotas for a more colorful demographic profile.

That particular brand of racial diversity, however, is good enough for affirmative action's champions. In their eyes, meritless pluralism is a magical quality that makes everything it touches infinitely better. What they participate in is a cult of diversity. Like adherents of the cults of antiquity that worshipped icons for their blessings, liberals today prostrate themselves before racial diversity. It is great and good and confers all kinds of neat things on those who embrace it, according to the primary arguments in favor of affirmative action.

The most important thing to remember is that the favored form of diversity isn't necessarily "the state of having people who are different races or who have different cultures in a group or organization," as Merriam-Webster would put it.[8] Diversity in today's America simply means having fewer whites around. Segregation, such as universities having racially exclusive dorms and events, is great as long as that racial exclusion doesn't mean "white only." An all-black dorm is a sign of diversity, but an all-white fraternity is a sign of Jim Crow. That double standard is easier to understand once you think of higher education's commitment to ethnic diversity as not one upholding the strict definition of the term.

Upholding affirmative action on the basis of ensuring sufficient ethnic diversity stems from a landmark 1978 Supreme Court decision. In *Regents of the University of California v. Bakke*, Justice Lewis F. Powell wrote on behalf of the majority opinion that racial preferences in college admissions were in keeping with the Constitution. Furthermore, in Powell's opinion, there was a compelling state interest in imposing diversity on campus. On a school having the goal of establishing a "diverse student body," the Supreme Court justice wrote that this was "clearly" constitutional.[9]

Powell stated that "the State has a substantial interest that legitimately may be served by a properly devised admissions program involving the competitive consideration of race and ethnic origin," and determined that giving a "plus" to minorities for their racial backgrounds in the admission process is an appropriate tool for this goal. According to Powell, "our tradition and experience lend support to the view that the contribution of diversity is substantial." This decision set the legal precedent safeguarding affirmative action and it is still the reigning argument for keeping the practice afloat today.

Though Powell issued the ruling that gave the green light for racial preferences in college admissions, he wrote that schools should not strive solely for ethnic diversity. He merely hoped racial background would be one of many factors that schools weigh in assembling a student body that can accurately represent America in all its hues, while ruling against explicit racial quotas. Racial preferences should be "narrowly tailored" for the sole purpose of maintaining sufficient diversity. But a court justice after Powell took a much stronger position in championing racial diversity as a compelling state interest in a decision that upheld the '78 ruling.

In 2003 the highest court in the land heard two cases challenging affirmative action, both of which were directed at the University of Michigan. The court ruled in favor of U of M in the case of *Grutter v. Bollinger*, but against the school in *Gratz v. Bollinger*. *Grutter* concerned Michigan Law School's consideration of race as a significant factor in its admissions process.[10] *Gratz* concerned the university's undergraduate admissions, which used an intricate points system that awarded a set number of points to minority applicants.[11] The court found the law school admissions "narrowly tailored" its employment of race to increase diversity, while its elaborate undergrad points system did not.

Justice Sandra Day O'Connor tendered the majority opinion in *Grutter*, which saved university race-based admissions. In O'Connor's opinion, a college having racial diversity "enriches" a student's experience at the school and affirms the school's justification for race-based admissions: "obtaining 'the educational benefits that flow from a diverse student body.'" O'Connor explicitly stated that the purpose of affirmative action was no longer to remedy past discrimination but to ensure that higher education attains the rewards of diversity. While the plaintiff argued that she was rejected from Michigan's law school due to her race and that the institution's policies amounted to racial quotas, O'Connor ruled that was nonsense. To the judge, the use of racial criteria in admissions, as long as it didn't come with specified quotas, was fine.

O'Connor did rule that these race-based policies should not be permanent and that they must come with a termination point. "It has been 25 years since Justice Powell first approved the use of race to further an interest in student body diversity in the context of public higher education. Since that time, the number of minority applicants with high grades and test scores has indeed increased . . . We expect that 25 years from now, the use of racial preferences will no longer be necessary to further the interest approved today," she said.

However, in a 2010 book essay, O'Connor walked back from her twenty-five-year deadline mandate and said there should be no set termination point for racial preferences in higher education.[12]

The man named as the defendant in both affirmative action cases, then Michigan president Lee Bollinger, unsurprisingly offered exemplary explanations for why college administrators are so committed to affirmative action both before and after the landmark decisions that made his surname famous. "Ethnic and racial diversity within a university setting is absolutely essential to the accomplishment of a university's missions, and is at the very core of what a university does," he declared at a 2002 law symposium. Citing Shakespeare, Bollinger argued that "cultural diversity" gives students the avenue to experience different points of view. "Grappling with race in America is, therefore, a powerful instance of, a powerful metaphor for, crossing sensibilities of all kinds, and crossing sensibilities is part of the core of Shakespeare's genius and of great education," he stated.

The college administrator went on to argue that the "the mere presence of a diverse group—women, minority, men, majority—affects for the better how we act and what we say, even without our knowing the personal viewpoints or opinions of the other people present." With that in mind, Bollinger admitted in this speech, "When an applicant's file reveals that he or she might add to the diversity of perspectives that are voiced in class, that helps the applicant's chances of admission."

Bollinger warned his audience that there would be a "devastating effect on [universities'] ability to assemble a diverse student body" if they are not allowed to consider race as a factor. To consider only socioeconomic factors would, according to him, overwhelmingly favor white people because that's the race of most poor people in America. Thus, the only way to achieve the proper form of diversity is to keep racial preferences in admissions.[13]

Sadly for Bollinger, the Supreme Court ruled against him in the Gratz case because his school's undergraduate admissions policies weren't "narrowly tailored" to fulfill those diversity goals. This legal setback had no effect on changing Bollinger's commitment to utilizing racial preferences to realize the ideal type of diversity. Writing in 2007, the now–Columbia University president says race-based affirmative action is terrific because it "foster[s] a greater spirit of community on campuses."

In the post-*Gratz* essay, he also argued against the notion that schools should just rely on test scores, high school grades, and extracurricular activities when it comes to admissions. "It is far less important to reward past performance—and impossible to isolate a candidate's objective talent from the contextual realities shaping that performance—than to make the best judgment about which applicants can contribute to help form the strongest class that will study and live together. For graduate schools and employment recruiters, that potential is the only "merit" that matters because in an "increasingly global world, it is impossible to compete without already knowing how to imagine, understand, and collaborate with a diverse and fluid set of colleagues, partners, customers, and government leaders," Bollinger said.[14]

So much for a color-blind meritocracy.

It is interesting that Bollinger would employ Shakespeare to bolster his defense of racial preferences when many of the beneficiaries of those policies now want to eliminate the Bard from basic courses. Apparently, Shakespeare's whiteness trumps his universal appeal to the modern campus agitator.[15]

College administrators and judges aren't the only powerful people who support race-based admissions policies—so does corporate America. In an amicus brief submitted for the Grutter case and cited by O'Connor in her majority opinion, General Motors argued "the future of American business and, in some measure, of the American economy depends upon" racially and ethnically diverse student bodies. "A ruling proscribing the consideration of race and ethnicity in admissions decisions would dramatically reduce diversity at our Nation's top institutions and thereby deprive the students who will become the corps of our Nation's business elite of the interracial and multicultural interactions in an academic setting that are so integral to their acquisition of cross-cultural skills," GM's brief declared.[16]

Multiple corporations sent two separate amicus briefs to the Supreme Court in late 2015 in anticipation of the legal body hearing a case concerning affirmative action. Signed by such powerful entities as General Electric and Wal-Mart, one brief contended that the companies "have found through practical experience that a workforce trained in a diverse environment is critical to their business success."[17]

With all these arguments in favor of college diversity and the tools to achieve it, there has to be a plethora of studies out there definitively proving this magnificence. One of the latest surveys aiming to prove the wonders of classroom diversity, however, undermines arguments in its favor. But it at least reinforces the image of diversity as the magic icon of twenty-first-century liberals.

Two academics—University of Texas at Dallas business management professor Sheen S. Levine and Columbia University sociology professor David Stark—offered their study on diverse work groups as a defense of racially based college admissions in a December 2015 *New York Times* op-ed. Their argument, as stated by the article's title, is "Diversity Makes You Smarter."

Their claim depends on what they found when they took a relatively small sample size of homogeneous and heterogeneous groups and pitted them against each other to effectively assess market price bubbles. According to the researchers, the diverse groups performed better than the non-diverse groups. Why? Because critical thinking increases from just having minorities around: "We wanted to understand whether the benefits of diversity stem, as the common thinking has it, from special perspectives or skills of minorities," they wrote of their intent. "What we actually found is that these benefits can arise merely from the very presence of minorities." Levine and Stark believe this mixture of races is good because it leads partners to question one another's analyses and views. "Diversity prompts better, critical thinking. It contributes to error detection. It keeps us from drifting towards miscalculation," the academics stated.

A school has a responsibility not to perpetuate racial preferences solely for the sake of correcting past discrimination and underrepresentation—it must do so to "promote sharper thinking for everyone." And it's not enough to have minorities on campus. According to Levine and Stark, every class on campus must have a sufficient level of diversity to make sure nobody is falling for "wrong ideas." It's an interesting legal question as to whether a school is barred from racial quotas at the application process, but can still implement them in the classroom. The authors seem to hope this discrepancy can be found both legal and morally right. The professors conclude their column with the modest boast, "Ethnic diversity is like fresh air: It benefits everyone who experiences it."[18]

But their claim of diversity's inherent intellectual stimulation dims when you consider the primary implication of their research: when surrounded by people unlike themselves, people forgo trusting one another. Rather than a sign of lively critical thinking, the friction caused by heterogeneous classrooms is a result of the breakdown of social trust that occurs within diverse communities.

Famed Harvard social scientist Robert Putnam, in his landmark 2007 study on social trust in America, found that communities with a high amount of diversity had little confidence in institutional leadership, trust both between and within ethnic groups was nearly extinct, and civic engagement registered in the doldrums. In other words, misery, apathy, anger, and atomization reign in diverse communities. Putnam, being a good liberal, was shocked by his own findings and sat on them for several years before publishing them. When he did finally publish them, he made sure to conclude his work with a call for coming to terms with diversity—even though he had just shown how miserable it made people.[19]

Regardless of Putnam's own opinion, his work illuminates why the diverse groups in Levine and Stark's study engaged in more "critical thinking": the participants were less likely to trust one another, which led to the friction the researchers reported as a positive. This tension may have worked out well in the isolated area of an academic study, but the results of it on a real-world campus or neighborhood aren't as pleasant.

"The more ethnically diverse the neighborhood you live in, the more you—every—all of us tend to hunker down, to pull in. The more diverse—and when I say all of us, I mean all of us. I mean blacks and whites and Asians and Latinos, all of us. The more diverse the group around us ethnically, in our neighborhood, the less we trust anybody, including people who look like us. Whites trust whites less. Blacks trust blacks less," Putnam explained to NPR at the time his study was published. "The only two things that go up as the diversity of your census track goes up are protest marches and television watching."[20] (While saying this in his interview, he pleaded that diversity would eventually bring everyone together—somehow.)

Along with Putnam's research on the socially corrosive effects of diversity, a Harvard Business study found that the mandatory diversity training implemented by many companies actually harms women and minorities because it tends to trigger bias and backlash against minorities. "Trainers tell us that people often respond to compulsory courses with anger and resistance—and many participants actually report more animosity toward other groups afterward," the researchers surmised. The study also found little evidence that the training improves diversity within the businesses that administer the programs.[21]

Sadly, though, hardly any of the young Americans filing into college every year have ever heard of the findings that undermine the cult of diversity. Moreover, it appears a great deal of them have embraced the cult themselves. According to a 2016 survey of Dartmouth University students, most of that Ivy League school's population prefers hiring nonwhite professors and admitting nonwhite students over white applicants, with African-Americans being the demographic most in favor of this attitude.[22] The survey also discovered that a majority of the students agree with the demand of campus Black Lives Matter supporters to expand the diversity of their university—even though the school already has a less white profile than that of America's general population.[23] The favored definition of diversity as a decrease or absence of whiteness is fully demonstrated by the Dartmouth study.

When the Tennessee state legislature voted to cut its university system's diversity funding in the spring of 2016, students staged protests at the Knoxville campus, and some even walked out of class. Defenses for the school's Office of Diversity typically included invocations of how "critical" money for "cultural awareness" was to the university. The executive of UT–Knoxville's student government issued a full-throated defense of maintaining the school's diversity funding, claiming the defunding bill, which "threatens the sustainability of an office that offers our campus such an integral piece of its identity is a threat to us all."[24]

Lawmakers failed to take into consideration these dire concerns, and voted overwhelmingly to strip the university system of diversity funding, in large part due to guidelines demanding gender-neutral language and encouraging students to stifle any "secret" Christmas party they find.

The curriculum and culture foisted upon students certainly play a part in why some of them are so devoted to the diversity cult. One public university recently voted to drop its math requirement for graduation at the same time it considered a stipulation that all students must take four classes that promote diversity to get their diploma.[25] But some schools might not be content with merely teaching the ideology to the students—they could want to require belief in it as a requirement of admission. Beginning in 2016, the University of Cincinnati—a public college, no less—demanded that faculty and staff applicants sign a pledge of commitment to "diversity and inclusion."[26]

It's only a matter of time before schools start requiring incoming students to sign the same pledge once the diversity cult feels its charges aren't progressing fast enough down the path of enlightenment.

The group that suffers the most from affirmative action

policies are arguably lower-income whites. As Lee Bollinger noted, having an admissions process that took into account socioeconomic status over racial identity would benefit whites more. And we can't have that now. Without the financial resources and the proper skin color to get into a good four-year university, millions of poor whites are denied their opportunity at the American Dream.

Former Democratic senator and onetime presidential candidate Jim Webb pointed out the unfairness of affirmative action in a 2010 *Wall Street Journal* column. He denounced policies that favored recent nonwhite immigrants who had never suffered discrimination in America while treating whites as one uniform bloc of folks. "The journey of white American cultures is so diverse (yes) that one strains to find the logic that could lump them together for the purpose of public policy," Webb wrote. He then mentioned how various white demographics— such as white Baptists—had been left behind over the years at the same time the government was expanding affirmative action to include all nonwhite ethnicities.

Calling the commitment to present affirmative action "misguided," he urged the federal government to maintain its policy of helping African-Americans overcome the past effects of discrimination while scrapping "government-directed diversity programs. Nondiscrimination laws should be applied equally among all citizens, including those who happen to be white," Webb asserted. "The need for inclusiveness in our society is undeniable and irreversible, both in our markets and in our communities. Our government should be in the business of enabling opportunity for all, not in picking winners. It can do so by ensuring that artificial distinctions such as race do not determine outcomes."[27]

Caucasians may appear to be the primary victims of affirmative action policies (and some of the defenders of racial preferences hope for that disenfranchisement), but that doesn't mean other groups don't suffer from the consequences as well. A significant number of Asian-Americans see racial preferences as wrongly excluding them from spots at the Ivy League, with some observers—such as tech developer and political commentator Ron Unz—going so far as to claim the New England enclaves maintain "Asian Quotas." This argument relies on data that show the number of Asians drastically growing in the United States, while their admission numbers at Harvard and other Ivies stagnate. In comparison with the California Institute of Technology, which relies on a more race-neutral, meritocratic admissions policy, the Asian student population has risen in line with their growth in the general population.[28]

Seeing these figures as strong evidence of discrimination, a coalition of Asian American groups filed a federal complaint in the summer of 2016 demanding an investigation into the admission policies of Brown, Dartmouth, and Yale.[29]

Unz postulates that not only do Ivy League policies discriminate against talented Asian students; they also serve to create a narrowing of the American elite by favoring the children of alumni and the well connected over those outside the confines of privilege. That's why poor whites who grow up in Appalachia are at a serious disadvantage in the admissions process compared to whites who attend prestigious boarding schools.

Affirmative action was implemented for African-Americans, and they remain its strongest defenders, but even they suffer negative consequences from racial preferences. According to "mismatch theory," many minority students, particularly

African-Americans, are accepted into competitive schools far out of the range of their skill sets and, in due course, struggle extensively during their time in college. This sense of failure leads to many nonwhite students feeling depressed and alienated, which can inevitably convince them to give up on college altogether or, if they stay, take up radical agitation. Richard Sander and Stuart Taylor Jr., the scholars who coined mismatch theory, believe minority students would be better served if they no longer had the advantage of racial preferences and went to schools based on their academic achievements instead of their skin color.[30]

But don't expect the acknowledgment of mismatch to take off anytime soon, judging by reactions to comments by the late Supreme Court justice Antonin Scalia during a 2015 court hearing. Merely mentioning that black students would have a better academic experience if they were accepted into schools suitable to their SAT scores brought a deluge of racism accusations upon the late conservative justice.[31] That's because the purpose of affirmative action is no longer to help the academic performance of anyone. It's there to achieve diversity—no matter the cost.

America once prided itself on its celebration of individual merit regardless of skin color, but that was before the cult of diversity became the religion of its most powerful figures. Now skin color trumps merit—as long as that skin isn't white.

2

POLITICAL CORRECTNESS IN THE AGE OF MICROAGGRESSIONS

Political correctness is one of the cardinal virtues of modern education. With universities so eagerly pursuing diversity, it is inevitable that colleges would create draconian speech codes to match the pace of change.

The college campus has long served as the willing vessel for setting the boundaries for what forms of speech are acceptable in polite discourse. The term *political correctness* first came to the fore of public consciousness at the dawn of the 1990s. Applied to the disconcerting ideological conformity sweeping over college campuses, PC became the preferred way to summarize what was wrong with higher education. If you were a conservative, of course. The *New York Times* defined political correctness in 1991, according to the trend's critics, as "a widespread tendency to use censorship, intimidation and other weapons abhorrent to the American political process to support popular demands for measures to enforce sexual, racial and ethnic equality."[1]

Stanford University was in many ways the epicenter of the generation X PC war. In 1988, the prestigious private university scrapped Western culture courses because they upheld a "European-Western and male bias."[2] Students protesting the oppressive curriculum requirements were joined by then Democratic presidential candidate Jesse Jackson in a famous demonstration where all participants chanted, "Hey, hey, ho, ho, Western Civ has got to go!"[3] And so did Western civ go.

The following year, the California-based school imposed a new policy that banned "racially offensive" speech after two inebriated students put Ludwig van Beethoven in blackface on a poster. The policy, naturally, resided on dubious constitutional grounds, and the university's stringent speech code was later overturned in a 1995 California state court ruling.[4] In spite of that one court ruling, the early '90s incarnation of PC pretty much got everything it desired.

Black studies, check. Gender studies, check. Elimination of Eurocentric curriculum, check. Multicultural centers and other goodies, check. The first iteration of outrage over campus political correctness didn't seem to stem the tide at all, besides spreading awareness of the problem.

Today, campus political correctness has morphed from its earlier triumphs into a more insidious phenomenon. College campuses still desire and retain the old PC ideology from the '90s, but now there is a greater determination to root out and suffocate speech deemed offensive. This latest outburst of political correctness comes at a time when a disturbingly high number of young adults favor suppressing "hate speech." According to the Pew Research Center, 40 percent of millennials support the government prohibiting viewpoints that may offend minorities. In comparison, only 28 percent of all Americans support that same position.[5] This feeling among the youth gives ample space for campus activists to agitate for censorship—and this intolerant spirit isn't just limited to public speech; private conversations on campus also face intense scrutiny.

Speech codes—reminiscent of Stanford's old policy prohibiting constitutionally protected, yet "offensive" expression—are still in place at various colleges nationwide. According to the Foundation for Individual Rights in Education (FIRE), a prominent advocate for student free speech, as of 2016 nearly 50 percent of American colleges had rules in place that curtail free speech.

FIRE's latest campus free speech report found college policies that seek to enforce legally questionable requirements of "tolerance" that basically ban offending anyone. Wesleyan University's policy on the matter states that all students have "the right to be protected against actions that may be harmful to the health or emotional stability of the individual or that degrade the individual or infringe upon his/her personal dignity." Several schools ban "hate speech" and stipulate punishment for "bias incidents." A bias incident, as defined by the speech code at Dickinson University, is "a pejorative act or expression that a reasonable person would conclude is directed at and/or impacts a member or group based on but not limited to those characteristics outlined above [namely, sexual orientation, gender identity, gender expression or legally protected characteristics such as race, gender, religion, national origin, ethnicity, disability or military status[6]]. A bias motivated incident can occur whether the act or expression was intentional or unintentional." Santa Clara University advises students that the best course of action if they experience a bias incident on campus is to dial 911.[7]

Another common free speech suppressant is the appropriately named "free-speech zone." A free-speech zone is an often-secluded area that is specifically designed to limit the free expression of students to that place alone. Nearly one in six colleges mandate free-speech zones, and they are often used to curb the speech of conservative activists on campus.

There are several egregious examples of students facing serious repercussions for violating these unconstitutional codes. Two students—one black, one white—at the Oregon-based Lewis & Clark College were placed on probation for an entire year in April 2014 after making racially sensitive jokes at a private party. During a game of beer pong, the black student named his team "Team Nigga" and the white student named his "White Power." The partygoers laughed over the exchange, but one passerby didn't find it funny and reported it to school officials.[8] In 2015 Colorado College suspended a student for two full years after he made a joke on the online commenting app Yik Yak about black women not being "hot." The private university deemed this act "abusive behavior" and claimed it caused a "disruption of student activities."[9]

While speech codes do encourage students to find offensive speech worthy of punishment, they are only a symptom of the larger politically correct culture of higher education.

Arguably, the defining trait of modern PC concerns is that of the "microaggression." A microaggression is any word, conversation, or action that could be construed as a denigration of a minority group by a member of a majority group. Microaggressions, according to the experts who believe in the concept, usually occur without any intent of perpetuating prejudice on the part of the microaggressor; they just come naturally to anyone affiliated with the so-called dominant culture. Following along with the theory, these subtle acts of discrimination marginalize minority groups from the dominant culture.

Microaggressions can come in multiple forms and be directed against all kinds of groups—except straight, white males, of course. According to Columbia University psychologist Derald Wing Sue, a noted racial microaggression researcher, there are three types of the misbehavior:

MICROASSAULTS: Conscious and intentional discriminatory actions: using racial epithets, displaying White supremacist symbols—swastikas, or preventing one's son or daughter from dating outside of their race.

MICROINSULTS: Verbal, nonverbal, and environmental communications that subtly convey rudeness and insensitivity that demean a person's racial heritage or identity. An example is an employee who asks a co-worker of color how he/she got his/her job, implying he/she may have landed it through an affirmative action or quota system.

MICROINVALIDATIONS: Communications that subtly exclude, negate or nullify the thoughts, feelings, or experiential reality of a person of color. For instance, White people often ask Latinos where they were born, conveying the message that they are perpetual foreigners in their own land.[10]

According to Sue, "microinsults and microinvalidiations are potentially more harmful because of their invisibility." In other words, the insults are so subtle that the offended fails to correct the offender and walks away with a severe emotional burden from the interaction.

Microaggressions have become a special obsession for both college administrators and perpetually outraged leftists. Multiple websites exist to document students experiencing these unbearable slights. Dozens of colleges have issued guides to students to be on the lookout for those uttering these snubs and often include microaggression awareness training in freshmen orientation.[11] The 2015–16 school year alone offered great examples of the kinds of words and phrases universities would like to banish forever.

The University of California–Los Angeles' "Recognizing Microaggressions" guide warned students to steer away from "color blindness" because it denies "racial and ethnic experience[s]." To remain politically correct, a student must always acknowledge a person's racial identity, according to UCLA's helpful guide. Other schools, such as the notorious University of Missouri, have also labeled color blindness (a person's claims to not see race) a manifestation of bigotry.[12] Several universities' microaggression guides went as far as to state that saying, "America is a melting pot" is offensive.[13]

How this advice on color blindness complements the standard leftist line that race is a harmful social construct is beyond my comprehension.

Other schools have found other benign phrases and mentalities that somehow happen to be secretly prejudicial. The entire University of California system issued a microaggression guide that included the example statements "America is a land of opportunity" and "The most qualified person should get the job."[14] The guide labeled these common phrases offensive because they "assimilate to the dominant culture." The University of Illinois, Urbana–Champaign funded an entire research project on racial microaggressions, which discovered some pretty damning cases of discrimination. According to the project, a classroom full of white people counts as a microaggression, as well as a minority student feeling "discouraged" during a meeting with an academic advisor.[15]

The University of New Hampshire's "Bias-Free Language" guide may be the high point of higher education's microaggression obsession, as it claimed the term "American" was itself "problematic." According to UNH's guidelines, saying, "American" to denote a U.S. citizen is a microaggression because it "assumes the U.S. is the only country" within the Americas. In addition to that basic term of our national consciousness, the public university advised students to also avoid saying "handicapped," "healthy," "rich," "poor," "fathering," and "mothering." All of those words promote outdated and hurtful notions about society, in the opinions of the politically correct administrators.[16]

Clearly, racial offenses aren't the only kinds of expressions that could fall under the microaggression category. A 2015 Harvard University report on the subject claimed female students face a daily barrage of sexist jokes and comments on campus. The result of microaggression prevalence for women and people of color is a "chilly" campus climate that causes serious psychological harm.[17]

Another set of problematic terms is gender pronouns. These ubiquitous words run the risk of hurting the feelings of young adults claiming they are a different sex from their biological one. Thus, some universities have advised students to choose "gender-neutral" pronouns to avoid offending their transgender peers. The University of Tennessee–Knoxville issued a directive at the beginning of the 2015 academic year that offered such bizarre words as "ze," "zhem" and "xyr" as alternatives for "he" and "she." "We should not assume someone's gender by their appearance, nor by what is listed on a roster or in student information systems," the directive explained. So to avoid offending a man who thinks he's a woman, UTK asked its students to use its alternative pronouns.[18]

Bear in mind, all of these examples come from taxpayer-funded public universities.

But the universities are not the most diligent enforcers of political correctness—the students themselves are. My *Daily Caller* colleague David Hookstead became public enemy number one at the University of Wisconsin in 2013 after he wrote an article for the school paper declaring that rape culture doesn't exist. He was peppered with threats of violence just for expressing a point of view.[19] The same thing happened at the University of Michigan when a writer for its main student newspaper satirized microaggression hysteria in a column for the campus conservative paper. He was fired from the main paper because his work created a "hostile environment."[20] Similar outrage followed a Wesleyan University student writing an essay in the *Wesleyan Argus* critical of Black Lives Matter in 2015. The one column resulted in the writer receiving a deluge of "racist" accusations, hundreds of copies of the paper that carried the article destroyed, and funding revoked for the *Argus*.[21]

And those are just examples of students who face the wrath of their triggered classmates. Speakers invited to share their viewpoints are also not safe from the fury of the social justice mobs. Two right-wing personalities toured across the country during the 2015–16 academic year to speak out against PC culture on college campuses. Conservative commentator Ben Shapiro and Internet provocateur Milo Yiannopoulos may be rivals, but both men when speaking independently on campuses were faced with the same degree of hatred. And both saw ridiculous examples of the kind of intimidation employed by campus agitators to silence speech they disagree with.

When Shapiro visited the campus of California State University–Los Angeles in February 2016 to give a talk on the costs of diversity, he was greeted with blocked doors, frequent interruptions, colorful jeers, and a pulled fire alarm. Attendees were threatened with violence by angry protesters, and Shapiro had to be escorted out under police protection due to the turbulence. Three months after the event, the school's president hosted a "healing space" for faculty and students to vent their frustration and mend the wounds of being "brutalized" by a conservative speaking on campus. "I get he's Jewish, so that's ironic that I'm calling him a neo-Nazi," one CSULA professor said of Shapiro, "but that's basically what he is. A neo-KKK member—let's call him that." CSULA president William Covino vowed to do everything in his power to prevent someone like Shapiro from speaking again on campus, but stated it was "very tragically and unfortunately" likely to reoccur.[22]

Milo Yiannopoulos faced a similar violent response to his May 2016 appearance at DePaul University as part of the flamboyantly gay writer's "Dangerous Faggot Tour." Protesters charged the stage, commandeered the microphones, and threatened Yiannopoulos for the crime of voicing a right-wing point of view. Outside the event, demonstrators assaulted a few attendees and even some unaware passersby. Unlike at Shapiro's CSULA event, security, which Milo paid out of pocket for, stood around and let chaos descend on DePaul's campus without raising a finger. The invited speaker tried to make the most of his event being disrupted and attempted a march all the way to the dean's office, before his crowd of supporters were turned away by the suddenly awake police.[23]

Fallout shortly ensued at DePaul with the school's president issuing an apology—for having allowed Milo on campus in the first place. "Generally, I do not respond to speakers of Mr. Yiannopoulos' ilk, as I believe they are more entertainers and self-serving provocateurs than the public intellectuals they purport to be. Their shtick is to shock and incite a strong emotional response they can then use to discredit the moral high ground claimed by their opponents. This is unworthy of university discourse," President Dennis H. Holtschneider wrote. While he did criticize the actions of the protesters, Holtschneider sympathized with their intent and compared their drive to that of the brave soldiers who stormed the beaches of Normandy.[24] But the apology letter did not save Holtschneider's job, and he resigned a few weeks after the Milo riot.[25]

In July, DePaul announced it had placed a ban on

Yiannopoulos ever speaking again on campus. A month later, it also banned Ben Shapiro from its environs.[26]

While conservative speakers are still willing to venture into campus safe spaces, many popular comedians—such as Jerry Seinfeld and Chris Rock—have given up on college crowds altogether. The reason: the kids are too politically correct to laugh at jokes anymore.[27]

Who needs administrators to regulate speech when activists will try to silence anyone they disagree with on their own?

With all of these egregious slights abounding on campus, how do colleges handle them besides issuing the mandatory guidelines? One tactic is, as mentioned earlier, the use of the "safe space," a trend that goes hand in hand with the microaggression obsession. A safe space is, in the words of a group advocating for the concept's existence, "a place where anyone can relax and be able to fully express, without fear of being made to feel uncomfortable, unwelcome, or unsafe on account of biological sex, race/ethnicity, sexual orientation, gender identity or expression, cultural background, religious affiliation, age, or physical or mental ability."[28] Considering how hard it is for a college to keep itself free of psychologically damaging snubs, creating a place where no one will feel offended seems like a very tall task.

But the difficulty of the goal hasn't stopped students and administrators from trying to create safe spaces on their campuses. The enactment of these offense-free zones typically coincides with speeches and events that traumatize students, and the safe spaces often, bizarrely, resemble kindergarten classrooms. Examples of this kind of behavior include feminists at Georgetown University constructing on-campus safe spaces in response to a fellow feminist, Christina Hoff Sommers, delivering a lecture entitled "What's Right (and Badly Wrong) with Feminism?" That speech was apparently liable, according to the feminist protesters, for traumatizing rape survivors with its content—even though it contained no apologies for rapists.[29] At Brown University, a 2014 debate on rape culture prompted the creation of an immensely well-stocked safe space for those who could not handle the subject matter of the event. That space offered traumatized students "cookies, coloring books, bubbles, Play-Doh, calming music, pillows, blankets, and a video of frolicking puppies."[30]

During the infamous November 2015 unrest at the University of Missouri, students made a safe space for those who were being "triggered" by all the flaky evidence of systemic racism on campus. The space was created right in the middle of a large demonstration against the school's administration for failing to address the institutional bigotry. When journalists trying to cover the protests tried to get into the safe space, they were harassed and threatened with physical violence for entering an area they were apparently barred from. Melissa Click, the professor who called for violence against an intruding journalist into the Mizzou safe space, soon became one of the most recognizable faces of campus insanity.[31]

For those unlucky students who may not have the opportunity to flee to a safe space when confronted with scary ideas, there's the trigger warning. A trigger warning is a notice placed before a text or some other content telling the audience that what may follow could cause discomfort among some readers or listeners. On a college campus, this tool has been taken to a ridiculous extreme in justifying the censoring of classic literary works on ludicrous grounds. For instance, distressed students at Columbia University have demanded the imposition of trigger warnings on Greek mythology because some of the tales "[marginalize] student identities in the classroom," according to an April 2015 op-ed published in the Ivy League school's newspaper. "These texts, wrought with histories and narratives of exclusion and oppression, can be difficult to read and discuss as a survivor, a person of color, or a student from a low-income background," the column added.[32]

The prevalence of trigger warnings and safe spaces within higher education has created an environment more suitable for toddlers than for adults. Both concepts accept that a significant number of college students are too mentally fragile to consume content they find frightening or offensive. Instead of challenging students to look beyond themselves and their own experiences, colleges offer the opportunity for blossoming adults to return to the stultifying cocoon of a sheltered childhood. The trend has become so ridiculous that prominent liberal commentators and scholars have come out to warn the country about the harmful effects of trigger-warning PC.

In a column for the *New York Times*, the left-leaning Judith Shulevitz expressed her concern for coeds "hiding from scary ideas." Shulevitz noted that college students of the past would object to speakers and curriculum not to their suiting on the basis of ideological conformity; now the students protest because they believe the offensive material puts them "in emotional peril." One of the reasons for this development, the *Times* writer explained, is that the claim of a medical trauma forces administrators to respond. All universities are required by federal law to ensure certain protected classes—such as women—are not subject to a "hostile environment." If a number of students claim some poor professor is promoting a "hostile environment" because he's teaching Homer without trigger warnings, a college dean is put into an unenviable bind. The argument inevitably gives crafty activists a valuable tool to use to achieve ideological goals.

Shulevitz pointed out that some legal theorists have justified this kind of coddling of offended students. According to these intellectuals, the Constitution is an inadequate protection for any speech that may cause "emotional injury" to young women and racial minorities. Shulevitz disagrees with the notion that some college students deserve this kind of protection at a college campus. "People ought to go to college to sharpen their wits and broaden their field of vision," she wrote. "Shield them from unfamiliar ideas, and they'll never learn the discipline of seeing the world as other people see it." Dismayed at the prospect, the journalist asks, "What will they do when they hear opinions they've learned to shrink from?"[33]

An influential long-form essay in the September 2015 issue of the *Atlantic* presents a more troubling product of this coddling: long-term psychological damage for students. No, not from the microaggressions themselves, but from campus PC culture. Written by free speech advocate Greg Lukianoff and social psychologist Jonathan Haidt, "The Coddling of the American Mind" insists the insanity currently besetting American campuses is different from past outrages. "It presumes an extraordinary fragility of the collegiate psyche, and therefore elevates the goal of protecting students from psychological harm," Lukianoff and Haidt wrote. "The ultimate aim, it seems, is to turn campuses into 'safe space' where young adults are shielded from words and ideas that make some uncomfortable.

And more than the last, this movement seeks to punish anyone who interferes with that aim, even accidentally. You might call this impulse *vindictive protectiveness.* "[34]

The authors argue that the overabundance of trigger warnings and safe spaces teaches students to think "pathologically" and resembles the developing causes for depression and anxiety. Instead of teaching critical thinking, colleges are increasingly encouraging students to develop cognitive distortions, which, according to the psychological theory upheld by Lukianoff and Haidt, leads to a myriad of mental illnesses. One of the main currents pushing the facilitation of cognitive distortions is higher education's embrace of emotional reasoning. The authors define emotional reasoning as discussion in which "your feelings guide your interpretation of reality." If something greatly upsets a young freshman, then there must be something gravely wrong with that particular item.

Other cognitive distortions that characterize current campus political correctness include fortune-telling ("you predict the future negatively"), catastrophizing ("you believe that what has happened or will happen will be so awful and unbearable that you won't be able to stand it"), magnification ("exaggerating the importance of things"), and mental filtering ("pick[ing] out a negative detail in any situation and dwell[ing] on it exclusively, thus perceiving that the whole situation is negative").

Lukianoff and Haidt take a very negative view of these developments and see them as a forecast of a dark future for the country. "Attempts to shield students from words, ideas, and people that might cause them emotional discomfort are bad for the students. They are bad for the workplace, which will be mired in unending litigation if student expectations of safety are carried forward. And they are bad for American democracy, which is already paralyzed by worsening partisanship," they wrote.

Both writers believe colleges should discourage the use of trigger warnings and rethink the skills and values they want students to imbibe during their four-year stay. But Lukianoff and Haidt think the most important step to ending the tyranny of microaggression hysteria is getting the federal government to change its byzantine policies on peer-to-peer harassment that pressure colleges into overreacting in response to nonsense.[35]

Quite naturally, the notion that the stereotypical college student is an overgrown child has served as an argument for why colleges need those constitutionally dubious speech codes. University of Chicago law professor and highly cited legal scholar Eric Posner has made that very same argument in defense of stringent university policies. "We are increasingly treating college-age students as quasi-children who need protection from some of life's harsh realities while they complete the larval stage of their lives," Posner wrote. "Many critics of these codes discern this transformation but misinterpret it. They complain that universities are treating adults like children. The problem is that universities have been treating children like adults."[36]

If that's the case, then the Chicago law professor believes it's required of the university to protect the college student from potentially harmful material as a parent would shield a child from an R-rated film.

Lost in all the discussion over whether students have the mental capacity of grade schoolers is the ideological motivation for the coddling and which students receive special protection. Shulevitz briefly alluded to the "vulnerable groups" calling for the censorship of offensive speech, but spent little time on the subject in her column. Lukianoff and Haidt hardly mentioned which groups are at the forefront of campus political correctness. In fact, their widely read article gives the impression that it is a common feature among all college students regardless of race, sex, and/or sexual orientation. Its cover image is that of a young white child in the garb of the frat boy Bluto from the movie *Animal House*, implying that administrators also coddle white males in fraternities.

That's not the case, however. Like all things pertaining to campus unrest, identity power politics are at the heart of this new iteration of political correctness. A white male crying out about reading *Hamlet* due to its distressing interfamily violence would not be taken seriously. A black female complaining about *Hamlet*'s troubling lack of nonwhite characters would be a very serious issue though. Remember: a microaggression can come only from a member of the so-called dominant culture. If the offended is not a part of the so-called dominant culture, then he or she is automatically the victim of the exchange. With a few notable exceptions, such as the Lewis & Clark case, minorities are virtually exempt from the dictates of campus PC.

Simply put, political correctness assigns more power to protected classes and stifles the speech of those who don't fall into a special category.

At least one prominent liberal is worried this trend may threaten America's vaunted political culture. Journalist Jonathan Chait, writing in a *New York* magazine essay, called the new form of PC an "undemocratic creed" that considers the race, gender, and background of a speaker the "very essence" of that individual's point of view. "Political correctness is not a rigorous commitment to social equality so much as a system of left-wing ideological repression," Chait wrote. He believes that while liberals like him understand that PC threatens to overturn the free exchange of ideas, it appeals to them because it presents "a more authentic and strident opposition to their shared enemy of race and gender bias."[37]

That kind of thinking is similar to the "repressive tolerance" outlined by the famous left-wing philosopher Herbert Marcuse more than fifty years ago. Marcuse, considered the godfather of "cultural Marxism" by many conservatives, believed there were two kinds of tolerance: one false and one true. The false form of tolerance is wrong because it allows for all forms of expression to go unmolested, which, in his opinion, leads to a tyranny of the majority. The true form of tolerance—deemed "liberating tolerance"—is right because it disenfranchises the "radically evil" opinions of the majority and grants more freedom to revolutionary minorities. "Liberating tolerance, then, would mean intolerance against movements from the Right and toleration of movements from the Left."

Marcuse went further, in the postscript to the essay, to explain his argument:

> I suggested in "Repressive Tolerance" the practice of discriminating tolerance in an inverse direction, as a means of shifting the balance between Right and Left by restraining the liberty of the Right, thus counteracting the pervasive inequality of freedom (unequal opportunity of access to the means of democratic persuasion) and strengthening the oppressed against the oppressed. Tolerance would be restricted with respect to movements of a demonstrably aggressive or destructive character (destructive of the prospects for

peace, justice, and freedom for all). Such discrimination would also be applied to movements opposing the extension of social legislation to the poor, weak, disabled. As against the virulent denunciations that such a policy would do away with the sacred liberalistic principle of equality for "the other side," I maintain that there are issues where either there is no "other side" in any more than a formalistic sense, or where "the other side" is demonstrably "regressive" and impedes possible improvement of the human condition. To tolerate propaganda for inhumanity vitiates the goals not only of liberalism but also of every progressive political philosophy.[38]

That extract perfectly encapsulates the mentality of campus activists who believe free speech and tolerance are concepts reserved exclusively for them—and there's no room for any "oppressive" opinions. The student activists clamoring for speech suppression are playing the role of Marcuse's revolutionary minorities in usurping power and setting the rules on campus. The campus demonstrator cloaks herself in moral superiority to achieve her ends. The speech she finds offensive can be excluded because she and her comrades claim it is "against our values"—meaning it is not in line with progressive orthodoxy. And so campus leftists are able to suppress all dissenting speech for the supposed good of humanity.

Lucky for them that 40 percent of millennials also agree that offensive speech should be banished.

3

VICTIMHOOD CULTURE

For ages, no one wanted to be a victim.

A victim was someone who was weak, humiliated, and powerless.

Even when someone had earned the distinction of victimhood after suffering from undeniable evil or a bizarre act of fate, the miserable man could not expect to earn a reward for his plight. Instead, dwelling on his victim status was more likely to let his peers know he was weak and existed at the bottom of the social totem pole. The victim card was an ineffective tactic against the aggressors who oppressed the poor soul. The victimizers were more likely to take it as a point of pride that they had dominated their prey, like a conquering army reveling in the anguish of their vanquished foes. The only reason an individual (or society) would publicize his victimization would be to justify his retribution against an aggressor.

That is no longer the case. Victimhood Olympics, in which multiple parties and individuals compete to prove that they are the most oppressed, now shapes public discourse in our time. Debates center around whoever can claim to have the most injustice done unto them and come out on top as the Gold Medal victim. Victimhood affords so much status in our society that there's become a cottage industry of hate crime hoaxes, all of which involve the fabulists broadcasting their made-up wrongs to win sympathy from the public.

On college campuses, students have burnished their victimization for all manners of causes. Those who shrieked over pro-Trump chalkings? They were victimized by the markings, and their safety was put at grave risk. Those offended by Mexican-themed fraternity parties and culturally appropriated Halloween costumes? Same deal.

These appeals to victimhood are not just a few isolated cases of social justice warriors spewing hyperbolic nonsense. The arguments they use to paint themselves as oppressed just to curry favor are expressions of a deeper change to the West's moral culture. In an illuminating study on microaggressions and campus life, sociologists Bradley Campbell and Jason Manning theorize that what we're seeing with college insanity is a transformation in our moral culture from one that prizes dignity as the highest virtue to one that values victimhood above all else.

According to Campbell and Manning, this change is most intensely felt at colleges, and one of the primary manifestations of this new victimhood culture is the fixation on microaggressions. The academic fad that condemns offhand comments as rank bigotry doesn't just freeze free speech and give free rein to identity politics. The two sociologists see the proliferation of websites, news articles, and scholarly essays on the subject as a form of social control to handle conflict on campus.

Websites dedicated solely to publicizing microaggression go through this tedious effort because they are dependent on third-party authorities to resolve these conflicts in the new moral system.[1] The exhaustive documentation of these perceived slights is done to prove they're a part of a larger pattern of injustice, which helps convince the disinterested third parties to take their side. When it comes to values, the microaggession sites see dominance as deviant behavior. "The grievances focus on inequality and oppression—especially inequality and oppression based on cultural characteristics such as gender or ethnicity. Conduct is offensive because it perpetuates or increases the domination of some persons and groups by others," wrote Campbell and Manning.[2]

Dominance is horrible, and victimhood is a sign of virtue. The worst trait one can have in a victim culture is "privilege," for it is the opposite of victimhood.

While the study's authors didn't mention it, the aggrieved see whites as their usual oppressors—particularly straight, white, male Christians. Campus agitators view them as hoarding all the power in society, and the insensitive jokes of whites are more than just the behavior of drunken frat boys. They reinforce an unjust system that favors people with light-colored skin.

The negative view of dominance within this value system encourages those who feel they are not in the dominant group to air their grievances against their opponents and further indulge in a particular kind of moral narrative.

> In the settings such as those that generate microaggression catalogs, though, where offenders are oppressors and victims are the oppressed, it also raises the moral status of the victims. This only increases the incentive to publicize grievances, and it means aggrieved parties are especially likely to highlight their identity as victims, emphasizing their own suffering and innocence. Their adversaries are privileged and blameworthy, but they themselves are pitiable and blameless.[3]

Of course, this victimhood is not assigned based on economic station or actual oppression. A daughter of a millionaire can be a victim, while the son of a struggling coal miner can be privileged. Status is dependent entirely on racial, cultural, and/or sexual identity.

Social interactions like this fit into the broader development of a victimhood culture, a moral system that is not just limited to ivory towers. Campbell and Manning define a culture of victimhood as

> one characterized by concern with status and sensitivity to slight combined with a heavy reliance on third parties. People are intolerant of insults, even if unintentional, and react by bringing them to the attention of authorities or to the public at large. Domination is the main form of deviance, and victimization a way of attracting sympathy, so rather than emphasize either their

strength or inner worth, the aggrieved emphasize their oppression and social marginalization. . . . It emerges in contemporary settings, such as college campuses, that increasingly lack the intimacy and cultural homogeneity that once characterized towns and suburbs, but in which organized authority and public opinion remain as powerful sanctions. Under such conditions complaint to third parties has supplanted both toleration and negotiation. People increasingly demand help from others, and advertise their oppression as evidence that they deserve respect and assistance. Thus we might call this moral culture a culture of victimhood because the moral status of the victim, at its nadir in honor cultures, has risen to new heights.[4]

This culture presents a marked contrast to earlier cultures of honor and cultures of dignity. Honor cultures were also characterized by an intolerance of insults. However, unlike victimhood cultures, honor societies prize individual dominance and the proving of one's physical bravery through violence. Honor is earned through a man's reputation among his peers. If a man is known for not answering insults and backing away from fights, his honor, which is dependent primarily on public opinion, diminishes. A known coward is the worst reputation one can have in an honor society. Men who prize their victimhood are not at all respected in honor cultures. Societies based on these values typically have weak authorities who are unable to resolve interpersonal disputes. Thus, the parties resolve the conflict between themselves on their own—even when their neutral third parties are available. An example of an honor culture would be America's frontier society, where state authority was limited and many conflicts were resolved through duels and vendettas.

As state authority expands and gains the respect of all who live under it, cultures switch from chiefly prizing honor to valuing dignity. Unlike honor cultures, which assign status based on public opinion, dignity cultures stress that individuals have intrinsic worth independent of what their peers think of them. Instead of drawing swords over an insult to one's wife, dignity cultures emphasize having a thick skin. Conflict is resolved through the authorities, and respect for the law is a high virtue. Self-restraint, rather than constantly testing one's physical bravery through one-on-one combat, is looked upon as a trait of a virtuous person. For most of the West's recent history, dignity culture has served as the dominant moral system and has gone hand in hand with modernization. Campbell and Manning cited 1950s small-town America as an exemplar of this way of life.

Changes since that time, however, have led to the growth of victimhood culture. The two sociologists argue that increasing diversity, atomization (breakdown of social connections and intimacy groups), demands for equality, and reliance on authorities to handle all disputes have laid the groundwork for victimhood to assert itself. According to them, cultural homogeneity was a key ingredient in maintaining America's dignity system. As that homogeneity began to evaporate, the foundations of dignity culture melted with it. The authors imply that to thrive, dignity cultures require their adherents to see their fellow citizens as within their own in-group, not as members of opposing tribes.

In contrast, victimhood culture depends on its subscribers to immerse fully into identity politics and for society to exist not as one harmonious whole, but as a rough patchwork of unrelated factions. Not shockingly, that makes conflict a predominant feature of social life. When it comes to disputes on campus between opposing groups, it is often a result of clashing moral cultures where both sides appeal to completely different values.

> What we are seeing in these controversies is the clash between dignity and victimhood, much as in earlier times there was a clash between honor and dignity. Looking at those clashes, we know that when contradictory moral ideals exist alongside one another people may be unsure how to act, not confident of whether others will praise or condemn them. . . At universities and many other environments in modern America the clash between dignity and victimhood engenders a similar kind of moral confusion: One person's standard provokes another's grievance, acts of social control themselves are treated as deviant, and unintentional offenses abound. And the conflict will continue.[5]

To outsiders who uphold the values of a dignity culture, the antics of a victimhood culture appear ridiculous and childish. But to those on the inside of campus culture, they are righteous outbursts against contemptible behavior. This conflict of values can go far in explaining why many older liberals are disgusted by what they see on campus while younger generations of the Left cheer it on.

Campbell and Manning indicate that some of these conflicts will arise between rival victim groups, with both sides appealing to the authorities to argue which faction has been insulted the most. They dubbed this "competitive victimhood."

One of the minority groups that best shows how victimhood culture works to their advantage and creates conflicts with other aggrieved parties are transsexuals. Twenty years ago, the thought that transvestites would one day become the cause célèbre for left-wing activists was at best a bad joke. The popular 1994 comedy film *Ace Ventura: Pet Detective* features a transsexual villain for laughs, letting Jim Carrey's character display his "female" nemesis's bulge to horrify the audience. Today, the film is held up as an example of the disgusting transphobia of the past and would have zero chance of seeing release from a Hollywood powerhouse.[6]

The defining moment for the cultural Left in 2015 was the celebration of Kardashian character Bruce Jenner's transformation into Caitlyn. Showered with awards and praise from every corner of the establishment, Caitlyn Jenner came to symbolize the ascent of the transgendered to the forefront of the Left's heroic victims. If you didn't agree with the hype or found "her" glamor shots unsettling, you were a bigot who perpetuated the oppression of the trans community.[7]

The feeling of supreme victimization among transsexuals comes with some unintended consequences though. The demand for all groups to recognize the unique suffering of the trans community comes at the expense of other groups' victimhood. One of the more ridiculous examples of this conflict comes, naturally, from a private liberal arts college in Colorado. In the fall of 2015, Colorado College attempted to screen *Stonewall,* a gushing film tribute to the riots that launched the gay rights movement. However, trans students at the college were not happy with the idea. In fact, they called the film "discursively violent" and condemned it for "reinforcing a hierarchy of oppression." The reason for this negative impression was that it did not feature enough nonwhite, lesbian, or transgendered characters—all while starring a white guy. In the end, trans activists demanded the cancellation of the pro-LGBT event because "the safety and well-being of queer and trans students surpasses the importance of a critical discussion."[8]

Eventually, administrators at Colorado College caved and indefinitely postponed the *Stonewall* screening. While ridiculous in its nature, the screening scandal illustrates how the *T* in LGBT is causing fissures in the gay community, particularly with lesbians and feminists. For instance, Miriam Ben-Shalom, a lesbian who gained fame for challenging the U.S. military's now-defunct ban on open homosexuals serving in uniform, was disinvited from a 2015 gay pride parade after making negative comments about transsexuals. Shalom is a strong believer that trans women can't truly be female because they have penises.[9]

This view is shared by more than a few feminists who see transsexuals as male insults to real "womyn." Feminist icon Germaine Greer has long voiced criticism of trans women and has declared, "You can hold a knife to my throat, I won't recognize trans people."[10] More diplomatically, Elinor Burkett, a former women's studies professor, wrote in a 2015 *New York Times* op-ed that transsexuals such as Caitlyn Jenner reinforce "harmful" gender stereotypes about women. To Jenner, what makes a woman is "a cleavage-boosting corset, sultry poses, thick mascara and the prospect of regular 'girls' nights' of banter about hair and makeup." To Burkett, what makes a woman is the life experience of being a woman, not the inner "feeling" a person has if he concludes he is the wrong gender.[11]

The embrace of the transgender cause as the hottest victimhood issue becomes particularly galling when experts persuasively argue that it has zero basis in science. Former Johns Hopkins University chief of Psychology Dr. Paul McHugh has written multiple essays explaining how sexual reassignment surgery is a terrible cure for what is likely a mental illness. Johns Hopkins was one of the pioneers in this surgery, which the psychologist found brought "no important benefits." "This intensely felt sense of being transgendered constitutes a mental disorder in two respects. The first is that the idea of sex misalignment is simply mistaken—it does not correspond with physical reality. The second is that it can lead to grim psychological outcomes," Dr. McHugh argued in a 2014 *Wall Street Journal* column.[12]

In a 2016 report he coauthored with University of Arizona biostatistics professor Lawrence Mayer for the well-respected *New Atlantis* journal, McHugh and his fellow expert similarly declared that the prevailing gender identity dogma had no basis in scientific reality: "The hypothesis that gender identity is an innate, fixed property of human beings that is independent of biological sex—that a person might be 'a man trapped in a woman's body' or 'a woman trapped in a man's body'—is not supported by scientific evidence." The scholars also found that promoting this mentality among children brings no value and can end up harming them if they pursue a reassignment surgery that they may wish to undo as they grow older.[13]

But a phenomenon that may just be a mental illness doesn't deter social justice warriors from celebrating those who think they are another sex as noble victims. The oppression they feel from traditional thinking on gender alone is enough to earn them support under a victimhood culture.

Victimhood culture is a phenomenon unique to twenty-first-century Western societies. However, a nineteenth-century philosopher detailed many of its distinguishing features long before it reared its head in gender-neutral guidelines.

The eccentric German philosopher Friedrich Nietzsche

didn't call this value system victimhood culture—he dubbed it "slave morality." Nietzsche has quite the reputation in the English-speaking world. Known primarily for his blunt, yet wrongly interpreted phrase "God is dead," he is seen as a harbinger for all kinds of awful things to both liberals and conservatives. To the American Right, he was a herald for the godless moral relativism that has eaten away at our institutions. To the American Left, he gave Adolf Hitler a philosophical basis for his monstrous agenda.

Neither of those impressions is quite accurate. Nietzsche was a complicated figure who frequently contradicted himself—sometimes in the same work. In spite of all his eccentricities and gadfly views, Nietzsche offered a sobering assessment of the development of moral cultures in his most cogent works, *Beyond Good and Evil* and *On the Genealogy of Morals.*

Rather than the three cultures of Campbell and Manning, Nietzsche pared his system down to two opposing moralities: master morality versus slave morality. Master morality bears similarities to honor culture, but not as close in relationship as slave morality is to victim culture. For instance, a notable difference between the philosopher's and the sociologists' systems is that master morality stresses an immunity to insults while honor culture is built on violent reactions to them. Slave morality, like victimhood culture, is rooted in a hypersensitivity to slights.

According to Nietzsche, master morality arises out of aristocratic cultures that prize martial skills, beauty, pride in action, and most important, power. The "good" and "bad" of a master morality amounts to what is noble and what is disgraceful. The rulers determine what is good, and the traits of their class are valued as the most honorable. Those at the bottom of society are "bad," and in turn, their characteristics are shunned. The nobles uphold power and "life-affirming" virtues. At the same time, the aristocrats despise cowardice, weakness, narrowness of utility, self-deprecation, and lying. Those who possess these qualities in an aristocratic society are contemptible and reside at the bottom of the social hierarchy.

Slave morality reverses this value system completely. Nietzsche argued that slave morality, like master morality, seeks to call those who articulate its tenets the good and right. The difference comes in who's promoting it, which he sees as emanating from the downtrodden in an aristocratic society.

> Suppose the violated, oppressed, suffering, unfree, who are uncertain of themselves and weary, moralize: what will their moral valuations have in common? Probably, a pessimistic suspicion about the whole condition of man will find expression, perhaps a condemnation of man along with his condition. The slave's eye is not favorable to the virtues of the powerful: he is skeptical and suspicious, *subtly* suspicious, of all the "good" that is honored there—he would like to persuade himself that even their happiness is not genuine. Conversely, those qualities that are brought out and flooded with light which serve to ease existence for those who suffer: here pity, the complaisant and obliging hand, the warm heart, patience, industry, humility, and friendliness are honored—for here these are the most useful qualities and almost the only means for enduring the pressure of existence.[14]

The "good" in master morality are evil, and those who are bad are actually good, according to slave morality. The German philosopher sees this fundamental difference in how the two value systems view power:

> Here is the place for the origin of that famous opposition of "good"
> and "evil": into evil one's feelings project power and dangerousness,
> a certain terribleness, subtlety, and strength that does not permit
> contempt to develop. According to slave morality, those who are
> "evil" thus inspire fear; according to master morality it is precisely
> those who are "good" that inspire, and wish to inspire, fear, while
> the "bad" are felt to be contemptible.[15]

Like victimhood culture, slave morality sees dominance as deviance and victimization as virtue. The privileged are not to be esteemed but hated for their ill-begotten power.

In master morality, the "bad" are treated without genuine hatred—they are merely pitiable. By the same code, enemies are desired in order to prove one's worth in life, but they do not necessarily fall into the "bad" category. They are just those with whom you come into conflict and are more likely to be fellow "good" nobles. In contrast, slave morality sees its enemies as pure evil. And the "evil" are terrible men who are only worthy of condemnation and persecution, not of respect and appreciation.

While the evil ones may be hated, Nietzsche deduces that "good" in a slave morality comes with a "touch of disdain." "The good human being has to be *undangerous* in the slaves' way of thinking: he is good-natured, easy to deceive, a little stupid perhaps."[16] Thus, a pitiable victim becomes the pinnacle of morality instead of the conquering warrior. Great achievements and awe-inspiring victories don't win you the label of "good." Only having the appearance of meekness will win you that honor, which is similar to how those at the pinnacle of victimhood culture earn their goodwill as well.

Nietzsche had a term for the displacement of old morals

in favor of new ones: the *transvaluation* of values. For the overturning of master morality by slave morality, he simply dubbed this transvaluation "the slave revolt." The underlying current behind this revolution is *ressentiment*, a French word used even in the original German. Similar to the English "resentment," Nietzsche describes ressentiment as the negative feelings the "inferior" retain within and project outward against some external antagonist. Instead of blaming oneself for one's problems, those with ressentiment want to blame an oppressor. College victimhood culture is the perfect example of this mentality in that it allows failing minority students to blame racism, rather than their lack of adequate study, for their bad grades.

The German philosopher astutely chronicles how this hostility begins to plant the seeds for the slave revolt in the *Genealogy of Morals:*

> The slave revolt begins when *ressentiment* itself becomes creative and gives birth to values: the *ressentiment* of natures that are denied the true reaction, that of deeds, and compensate themselves with an imaginary revenge. While every noble morality develops from a triumphant affirmation of itself, slave morality from the outset says No to what is "outside," what is "different," what is "not itself"; and *this* No is its creative deed. This inversion of the value-positing eye—this *need* to direct one's view outward instead of back to oneself—is of the essence of *ressentiment*: in order to exist, slave morality first needs a hostile external world; it needs, physiologically speaking, external stimuli in order to act at all—its action is fundamentally reaction.[17]

Eventually, the "slaves" take on traits that enable them to outwit the masters. "The values of the weak prevail because the strong have taken them over as devices of leadership," the philosopher wrote in his uncompleted *The Will to Power* on how the transvaluation takes root.[18]

Nietzsche described the primary virtue of the slaves as the "vengeful cunning of impotence," which clads

> itself in the ostentatious garb of the virtue of quiet, calm resignation, just as if the weakness of the weak—that is to say their *essence*, their effects, their sole ineluctable, irremovably reality—were a voluntary achievement, willed, chosen, a *deed*, a *meritorious* act. This type of man *needs* to believe in a neutral independent "subject," prompted by an instinct for self-preservation and self-affirmation in which every lie is sanctified. The subject . . . has perhaps been believed in hitherto more firmly than anything else on earth because it makes possible to the majority of mortals, the weak and oppressed of every kind, the sublime self-deception that interprets weakness as freedom, and their being thus-and-thus as a *merit*.[19]

The dependence on a "neutral independent subject" for moral sanction echoes the need victimhood culture has for a powerful third party to resolve conflict in its system. Morality can only be doled out by an external power above the community one belongs to. The "good" in victimhood and master moralities do not deal out the justice themselves, as they would in an honor culture. It is always up to a higher power, to whom the good must make their appeals.

Nietzsche applied the master-slave morality paradigm in ways to which some readers may object, and he articulated a variety of positions that would strike us today as very strange. However, those qualms do not disqualify his insight into a phenomenon now taking shape within our own society—all formulated in works published well over a hundred years ago.

Oddly enough, though, a fair number of conservatives like to blame Nietzsche himself for planting the root of the West's moral rot. When assessing the inversion of the value system of traditional bourgeois society—with all its corresponding adoration of transsexuals and other bizarre characteristics—conservatives frequently point the finger at "moral relativism." The founder of modern American conservatism, William F. Buckley, derisively defined moral relativism as the idea that "what's right for you may not be right for me," and attributed this way of thinking to his liberal foes.

Writing in *National Review,* which Buckley founded, Jonah Goldberg described the decadence of pop culture as a "triumph" of Nietzsche's particular brand of moral relativism. "When I talk of the triumph of Nietzsche, all I mean is that do-it-yourself morality, informed by personal passion rather than old-fogey morality, is the new norm," Goldberg wrote.[20]

The popularity of Nietzsche bashing among conservatives can be traced back to Professor Allan Bloom's famous 1988 tract against higher education, *The Closing of the American Mind.* Bloom dedicated an entire chapter to condemning the "Nietzscheanization of the American Left" and how it left progressives embracing relativism and nihilistic hedonism.[21]

But not all conservatives agree on the evil of Nietzsche. Conservative political theorist Paul Gottfried has argued at length about the worth of the German philosopher's writings to those on the American Right and has dismissed the criticisms that he was grandfather of the hippie Left.[22] Even Jonah Goldberg has admitted that Nietzsche's concepts are valuable for understanding

PC culture, especially the concept of ressentiment.[23]

The assessment that moral relativism is responsible for the malaise plaguing Western society completely misunderstands the Left. The modern Left is animated by an intense sense of moral righteousness, not by a laissez-faire attitude toward different lifestyles. Christian bakers who refuse to make cakes for same-sex couples are bigots. Conservative students who want to host an antifeminist speaker are shut down and harassed. For there to be a "do-it-yourself morality," a level of respect must be afforded to different viewpoints and ways of life. That's not the case in America today.

Along with the lack of respect for those who don't kowtow to progressive orthodoxy, there is the underlying desire to have everyone share the same beliefs. We all must acknowledge the bravery of Caitlyn Jenner's sex transition. We all must think Black Lives Matter has a point. We all must think our country depends on mass immigration to survive. This is not moral relativism; it's postmodern Puritanism. Just like the colonial Calvinists who settled Massachusetts, social justice warriors (SJW) are dogmatic, self-righteous, and intolerant of different views. They demand conformity, and they love witch hunts. They even have their own form of original sin: being born white, which requires constant atonement. The SJWs just aren't that concerned with churchgoing and modest dress, as their Puritan forebears were.

Changes to our moral culture are not a result of a growth of relativism. They result from a rival value system challenging the old dignity culture of America's past. If you are a victim, you are now a hero thanks to our society's transvaluation of values.

Within both Nietzsche's slave morality and Campbell and Manning's victimhood culture, those at the top of the previous moral culture were hated for simply existing at the top. The only way for the powerful to redeem themselves is to check their privilege and submit to the moral superiority of those trodden underfoot by the old hierarchy. The oppressed then become the ones in charge and create a new system to justify their own superiority.

Campbell and Manning never spelled it out in their study, but the desire for taking power is an obvious motivator for those who seek to erect a victimhood culture. Those at the bottom can now reach the top when their past status becomes a virtue. That's why the moral culture of victims goes hand in hand with the identity politics that dominates higher education.

4

IDENTITY POLITICS

America is no longer a homogeneous nation. Innumerable groups—of all races and creeds—live within its borders and challenge its history. Multiculturalism has risen to destroy America's link to Western civilization. Diversity is preached as the highest good, alongside equality.

Predictably then, identity politics is an inescapable feature of American society. Our pluralistic character is largely responsible for this. The possibility that different groups living among each other would compete for power and privileges is a fact of life, especially if there is little that brings them together. So the people turn toward a whole variety of particular identities to give them a sense of belonging and status.

Everybody has a background that shapes who they are, how they are viewed by their peers, and how they make decisions. A person can be defined by any number of traits and characteristics. It can be either something as fixed as one's race and gender, or by freely chosen attributes, such as political affiliation and religion. An identity groups an individual with others who share that same identity, particularly if a society is keen on categorizing its members along certain lines. If class structure is rigid and determines status in a society, class identity becomes important. Same goes with race and ethnicity. When the ties that bind a society together weaken, people will seek to place themselves in separate groups rather than in the national body as a whole.

In diverse, tolerant, postmodern America, there's a whole host of identities for a person to choose from to earn status in our society. Your race, your ethnicity, your "gender identity," your sexual orientation, your disability—all can be used to define you and place you in a special category outside the dominant majority. America's particular brand of identity politics is designed to gain power for minority groups at the expense of either the majority or rival constituencies.

The one identity that's disadvantageous in our society is that of that awful dominant majority. If you're a white, straight, Christian, "cisgender" (identified by the gender you were born with) male, don't expect your identity to do much for you in our climate of "identitarian" power struggles. This double standard plays out routinely in higher education. At the start of the fall 2016 semester, a "Welcome White Week" prank poster at

Northern Kentucky University drew a very different reaction from the event it was intended to mock: NKU's Welcome Black Week. Protests erupted over the poster, which simply changed the race being welcomed. "Racism and discrimination must go! We will not stand for the undermining and the deliberate disrespect of our struggle. OUR VOICE WILL BE HEARD!" exhorted one of the incensed black students.[1]

The same thing happened the year before in response to the creation of multiple "White Student Union" Facebook pages following high-profile demonstrations at the University of Missouri and other schools. Some were created by avowed white nationalists, but most of the group pages were made by ordinary students who wanted to strike back at out-of-control identity politics. Since the word "white" was used in the names of these pages, it naturally elicited charges of racism—even though nearly every college in America has a Black Student Union and other ethnocentric entities.[2]

Identity politics focuses solely on serving group interests and is fundamentally shaped by the understanding that there are interests unique to those particular classifications. It does not judge a person based on his or her qualities as an individual, but on which group that person falls into. It overturns the American ideal of individualism and replaces it with bitter tribalism.

The recent madness at college campuses is only an extreme version of what we're seeing in society in general, and a possible indicator of what lies in store for the country's future. Black Lives Matter activists demanding that more African-American professors be hired to better improve racial awareness is identity politics. Feminists demanding the overturning of due process in sexual assault cases is identity politics. Hispanics wanting curriculum changes to better portray their preferred version of ethnic history is identity politics.

There's arguably no place where this political style influences the daily lives of its participants more than a college campus. To understand how identity politics work, you have to understand what it's not.

For one, it is not the kind of politics envisioned by the Founding Fathers and classical liberals. The view of politics as one of reasonable discussion and the free exchange of ideas between individuals who agree on basic principles is not upheld in the arena of identitarian struggle. Compromise is either scorned or is a pleasant euphemism for absolute capitulation. It's hard to discern the same set of shared values when one side appeals to reason and the social justice warriors brandish forth race, gender, and oppression in a stew of emotional hysteria.

"Agree to disagree" isn't the motto here. It's "I win, you lose."

The zero-sum game of identity politics, which pits different groups together in a vicious competition for power, has far more in common with the political theories of the German legal scholar Carl Schmitt than it does with classical liberalism. Schmitt imagined politics not as reasonable discussion, but as hostile warfare. The fundamental distinction in politics, according to Schmitt, is who counts as a friend and who is an enemy.

Equating the categorization of good and evil in morality with beauty and ugliness in art, Schmitt wrote in his 1927 opus, *The Concept of the Political*, that the friend and enemy distinction is the simplest way to understand political actions and motivations. The political enemy, he argued, was not a personal one, but a public foe, one who is an opponent for reasons of group completion, not because of private animus.

The distinction of friend and enemy denotes the utmost degree of intensity of a union or separation, of an association or dissociation. It can exist theoretically and practically, without having simultaneously to draw upon all those moral, aesthetic, economic, or other distinctions. The political enemy need not be morally evil or aesthetically ugly; he need not appear as an economic competitor, and it may even be advantageous to engage with him in business transactions. But he is, nevertheless, the other, the stranger; and it is sufficient for his nature that he is, in a specially intense way, existentially something different and alien, so that in extreme case conflicts with him are possible . . . Each participant is in a position to judge whether the adversary intends to negate his opponent's way of life and therefore must be repulsed or fought in order to preserve one's own form of existence.[3]

The friends and enemies that Schmitt described were nation-states, not student coalitions at your local college. In spite of that intention, the theory can be applied to present trends in American society and our increasing Balkanization. An enemy doesn't need to be a country with whom your homeland is at war; it can be another identity group living in the same society as you.

On a college campus, the desire to attain the power and privileges bestowed by the university can pit various minority groups against one another over issues such as which cultural center receives more money. However, that's not what America's identity politics revolves around—it's minorities united against the majority. A specified minority group is any protected class that is labeled an oppressed element of society. The enemy is the straight white male, who's doing all the oppressing. The shared cause for groups as different as black nationalists and lesbian feminists is hatred for traditional Western society—a society they perceive as fundamentally rooted in white supremacy and other chauvinistic attitudes.

To redress these historical wrongs, they assail the old institutions to coerce them to give these minority groups special accommodations and rewards. Unlike the friend-and-enemy battles between states, it's not the stronger party overpowering the weaker one. It's actually the opposite. These groups appeal to their status as powerless victims in order to gain prestige and advantages over their opponents. Their rhetoric fits perfectly into the victimhood morality that reigns over college campuses and allows them to wage war against their wicked foes without restraint. Rather than conquering the majority, these minorities seek to retain their enemy as their patron—albeit, one that is the moral inferior. The destruction of the evil white man isn't the goal; it's his acceptance of white guilt and privilege that's the objective. If the former ruler accepts that status, then he is more likely to strive to rectify every perceived injustice and bow before the moral superiority of the protected classes.

Identity politics, as it is practiced on a college campus, is strictly an antiwhite phenomenon. The majority is barred from copying the kind of tactics employed by Black Lives Matter because Caucasians are still in charge. White identity politics is white supremacy, so the enemy of these activists is forced to play by a different set of rules. In fact, the enemy doesn't really see itself as a group, or even their opponents as menacing tribes.

Many of the targets of the campus identitarians are god-honest liberals who believe in all the things a right-thinking progressive is supposed to be. Yet, they're classified as oppressors due to their skin color and positions of authority.

Take for example the pitiable case of Nicholas Christakis. Christakis was your standard liberal Yale University professor and housing dean before fall 2015. Then he had the audacity to defend his wife—a fellow Yale administrator—who argued that students shouldn't get so upset over Halloween costumes. Christakis suffered a public humiliation from an impromptu student kangaroo court on campus grounds for that position. His primary inquisitor was a black female student who berated him for threatening her safety as a minority by supporting a person's right to wear any Halloween costume he or she sees fit (rather than struggling to avoid "culturally unaware or insensitive choices"). She, along with her cohorts, demanded Christakis and his wife, Erika, step down from their positions for failing to uphold the right of minority students to live without being offended. The Christakises tried to defend their position by stating how much they support racial justice and couching their argument in progressive language—to no avail.

Both man and wife took the next semester off from teaching and eventually announced their resignations from overseeing the Silliman College at Yale a few months after they were cast as white oppressors.[4]

Hapless white liberal administrators and professors find themselves in similar positions when dealing with the fury of campus agitators. Appeals to past support for progressive causes and liberal values fall on deaf ears with their accusers. Skin color and identity matter more than shared political principles in the toxic climate of contemporary campus activism—a fact that should terrify the older crowd of liberals. As implied by Schmitt's friend/enemy distinction, abstract political principles fall before the power of the tribe. Campus identity politics is no exception.

Another demographic that is starting to come under the crosshairs of campus identitarians are Jews. Due to the prevalence of anti-Israel sentiment among the hard-core Left, Jewish people are finding themselves pushed out of safe spaces. Pro-Palestinian groups, such as the Boycott Divestment and Sanctions movement and Students for Justice in Palestine, frequently engage in anti-Semitic behavior on campus, such as shouting slurs at Jewish onlookers during protests and demanding the rejection of Jewish candidates for student government.[5] Even the Jewish allies of minority identity politics find themselves the brunt of the agitators' rage. Two Jewish attendees of the University of California Student Association's 2015 Students of Color Conference witnessed public avowals of Holocaust denial and apologetics for terrorism against Israeli civilians. "I was made to feel uncomfortable and unwanted in a space that was meant to be inclusive and safe," one of the attendees said of the event. "It was in that moment, during that conference, that I realized that every identity and every intersection of identity was to be welcomed and championed in progressive spaces—except mine."[6]

There are a plenty of reasons why this primal mentality is taking over the minds of a significant number of young people. Colleges prize racial and other identities in admission policies. If being black got you a prestigious scholarship, why not go further and embrace that trait as the core element of your identity? The college experience further elevates the minority consciousness of students with entire studies, departments, and organizations dedicated to fomenting the seeds of radical identity politics. Student groups such as the Black Student Union emphasize membership reserved exclusively for adults of a certain background and openly advocate solely for that group's interests.

Black studies, women studies, Chicano studies, queer studies, and other enriching curricula all serve to inculcate students with a sense of status outside of the mainstream and place eager learners into their own special group. Moreover, these identity-based studies are promoted as an antidote to the supposed majority chauvinism of normal courses. Unsurprisingly, animosity toward whites is not an unusual feature of these classes.[7]

The blame for the allure of identity politics does not fall entirely on the shoulders of American higher education, however. In the nation as a whole, this situation is an outgrowth of the contemporary view of the United States. America is unique among nations in that it has to routinely debate its identity. The current elite consensus is that we are a proposition nation founded on abstract ideas, not on an organic identity. Republican Speaker of the House Paul Ryan voiced this very sentiment in a rebuke to Donald Trump during the Republican Party's 2016 presidential primary. "America is the only nation founded on an idea—not an identity. That idea is the belief that the condition of your birth does not determine the outcome of your life," Ryan declared, before stressing that America's leaders had always come together through compromise and sensible debate. That's because we all believe in the same ideas.[8]

To anyone who may wonder why our country is rife with bitter partisanship if we really do all share the same values, there's an obvious explanation: we don't all share the same values. Of course, every American believes that anyone can succeed no matter one's status is at birth. But is that belief at the core of every American's worldview? Is that enough to keep us united as a nation? Is it enough to inspire young men to fight and die on its behalf?

Smart people on both sides of the political aisle seem to think so, and we offer up equal opportunity as the foundation of the "American Creed" that defines the nation. The famed sociologist Gunnar Myrdal, who helped popularize the term, said that American history is the story of "the gradual realization of the American Creed." Myrdal believed that the values of liberty, equality, rule of law, and fair treatment of all people were the glue that kept the nation's "melting pot" together.[9] There are numerous flaws with this view of American identity, and the best argument against it is found in the late political scientist Samuel Huntington's final tome, *Who Are We?* In the context of campus identity politics, the two most serious flaws in this "creedal nationalism" are its inability to provide much of a basis for a strong identity and its susceptibility to attacks from the Left.

While most Americans uphold the values associated with our ascribed creed, it says little about where they come from and who they are. Samuel Huntington cherished the American Creed, but believed it wasn't enough to sustain a strong national culture. Strong identities give a people a sense of meaning in their lives and a place in the world. The American Creed offers a nice set of platitudes, but little in the way of history and culture. It imagines the only thing Americans have in common is the desire to make money free of government restriction. On the other hand, the racial and gender identities offered up by college professors provide students with culture, history, and meaning to themselves. A radical philosophy such as Afrocentrism offers minority students a more exciting alternative than the bland and cultureless American Creed.

Huntington believed that the creed did in fact come from

a strong national culture, not out of thin air. The Anglo-Protestant culture he described glowingly in his book offered Americans a sense of meaning, shared values, and a connection with one another. It emphasized English as the spoken language, hard work, piety, and individualism.[10] Unfortunately for Huntington, this national identity has become out of fashion because it excludes other cultural forms and is too rooted in the bad old America. The new America is multicultural and only likes the ideas created by Anglo-Protestant culture, but not the culture from whence those ideas originated.

In addition to the enticing options afforded those who can demonstrate their difference from the historic American nation, there are the curricula and ideas that preach contempt for the ideals and past of the United States and Western civilization. Two generations raised on Howard Zinn's *A People's History of the United States* are not going to look back fondly on the American past. With that tainted history comes the veneer of false ideals. All the platitudes about equal opportunity in the United States are just lies to the ears of the young agitator ready to dismiss the pabulum of the creedalists at a moment's notice. Identity politics doesn't accept the inherent righteousness of American ideals because too many people were excluded from those wonders. All too often, they were just empty words uttered to buttress an unjust system—an unjust system forged by white Christian males, no less.

Since none of the Founding Fathers were nonwhite, female, non-Christian, or into alternative lifestyles, the values they enshrined at this nation's creation are seen as inherently tainted. For something to be taken as good and right among the campus Left, there must be a sufficient level of diversity. All that dreadful whiteness of the Constitutional Convention makes what those men created wrong from the start. In the realm of minority identity politics, ideas and principles cannot stand on their merit alone—who's behind them is the more important matter. If a bunch of white men come up with something with no minorities in the room, then whatever they come up with—no matter how great—is fundamentally awry.

That's why some of the towering figures of American history are finding themselves removed from college campuses. Thomas Jefferson may have laid the foundations for this country in the Declaration of Independence, but that's not enough to keep him safe at your local college. Who else but the notorious University of Missouri who lead the charge in the effort to get rid of Jefferson statues from campus safe spaces? Activists at the school started a petition to remove the third president's statue from the Columbia-based school's confines in October 2015 and decked out the figure in sticky notes labeling him a "racist" and a "rapist." "It's a symbol of violence to many students," petition organizer Maxwell Little said of the statue. "We talk about wanting to fix the culture of sexual violence and racism on campus, but that sits here. What really are the values of the University of Missouri?"[11] Apparently, not the same values that guided the Founding Fathers.

Jefferson's alma mater, William and Mary College, witnessed similar vandalism of its statue honoring the great man. Again, sticky notes declaring him a rapist and a racist dotted his metallic façade.[12] At the University of Virginia, the school Jefferson founded, several professors and students asked the college's president in 2016 to stop quoting the Founding Father because it undermines "equality."[13] Multiple-state Democratic parties have renamed their traditional Jefferson–Jackson dinners for the same reasons campus leftists post sticky notes on the founder's statue.[14] The man who articulated the ideas and values that have guided America for generations is irredeemable because he was a typical man of his class and time. Jefferson owned slaves and had illegitimate children with a favored slave, just as many men of his day did. That doesn't make it right, but it certainly doesn't negate his contributions to the world. Identity politics, however, can't get over the author of the Declaration of Independence being an evil white slave owner and demand his expulsion from public life.

Jefferson, of course, isn't alone in becoming a target of social justice warriors. There are obvious figures who come under fire, such as John Calhoun, who argued slavery was a "positive good."[15] But there are less obvious ones who also face increased scrutiny, such as progressive icon Woodrow Wilson. Students at Princeton University, Wilson's alma mater, staged sit-ins and marches in the fall of 2015 to urge the Ivy League school to immediately rename all buildings bearing the twenty-eighth president's name. The anger was not over Wilson supporting the League of Nations or endorsing a very broad reading of the Constitution. It was because he supported segregation, at a time when most men of his stature did as well. "Why do we even care about Woodrow Wilson at this juncture?" asked one upset student. "Because a lot of time that you are walking around this campus and you feel like you don't matter . . . the reason is because his legacy is sticking around these walls."[16]

But a historical figure doesn't even need to have black marks to his record to catch the fury of campus crazies. He just needs to be white. Agitators at Yale University demanded the elimination of a poetry course that featured too many white male writers. The Major English Poets course has been a staple at the Ivy League school since 1920, and it skews "too white" simply due to the reality that most of the people who wrote English poetry are, shockingly, white men. Students wanted it gone for that very reason, as explained by the online petition seeking its termination. "A year spent around a seminar table where the literary contributions of women, people of color and queer folk are absent actively harms all students," the petition confidently asserted.[17] Chaucer and Shakespeare—in spite of their historical significance, beautiful verses, and stories that transcend time—are not welcome in a required college course solely because of their skin color.

This mentality is why the creed and an American identity based exclusively on abstract principles hold little appeal for the campus agitator. Just ask the members of Movimiento Estudiantil Chicanx de Aztlán (MEChA), a student movement committed to expressing Chicano ethnic pride and unifying the Mexican-American community on campuses nationwide. This group has zero desire to assimilate into the American nation but works explicitly to maintain a separate cultural identity among Chicanos. "Chicanismo results from a decision based on a political conscious-ness for our Raza, to dedicate oneself to building a Chicana/Chicano Nation. Chicanismo is a concept that integrates self-awareness with cultural identity, a necessary step in developing political consciousness," MEChA's mission statement declares. "Chicanismo involves a personal decision to reject assimilation and work towards the preservation of our cultural heritage."[18]

A large element within MEChA advocates for the *recon-quista* of the American Southwest, or as they call it, Aztlan.

"The ultimate ideology is the liberation of Aztlan. Communism would be closest [to it]. Once Aztlan is established, ethnic cleansing would commence: Non-Chicanos would have to be expelled—opposition groups would be quashed because you have to keep power," a MEChA chapter leader was quoted as saying. The group expresses Latino racial pride and embraces the slogan "For La Raza todo. Fuera de La Raza nada" ("For the Race, everything. Outside the Race, nothing").[19] MEChA is not some fringe outlier—it boasts chapters all across the United States and has a strong presence throughout the Southwest. The identity politics that dominate a college campus make it possible for a group dedicated to anti-Americanism, ethnic chauvinism, and splitting up the Union to find an all-too-welcoming home.

Particularly when your average American history course teaches students that our country cruelly stole land from Mexico and oppressed every nonwhite group under the sun.

The great tragedy of creedal nationalism is how much its believers cling to it as a superior idea to the racism and ethnic chauvinism of other nationalism, yet the vanguard of the Left still views it as coded white supremacy.

The negative curriculum reinforces a marked skepticism to rhetoric about the exceptionalism of the nation. When it's considered problematic to think of America as the "land of opportunity" in the opinion of various college guidelines, the creedal identity is not quite the strongest rhetorical weapon to win over the campus crowd. And just imagine if students were asked of America as an organic cultural unit.

There's a strong case for emphasizing a different kind of national identity that stresses a shared history and a basis in the Anglo side of Western civilization—the identity Americans previously cherished and challenged immigrants to assimilate to, one that could give a sense of place to its citizens and unite them into a harmonious whole. Instead, we have an academic orthodoxy that sees that idea as rank white supremacy and prefers to offer history as seen through the eyes of myriad identities. Unsurprisingly, the youth reading those books imbibe their teachings and embrace the struggle of identity politics in opposition to the old America.

5

GUILTY OF BEING WHITE

Slavery. Segregation. The Ku Klux Klan.

Those are just some of the cheerful topics that may come to mind for a young campus activist when she thinks of race relations between whites and blacks—especially if she's reading the popular takes on race in America, such as Ta-Nehisi Coates's massive best seller *Between the World and Me*.

Undoubtedly, America has had a tumultuous racial history, and the treatment of its black denizens has, historically, been at best shameful and at worst inhuman. But fortunately, America has striven over the last sixty years to correct the sins of the past. Segregation was eliminated. Racist terrorism is met with the full brunt of the law. Opportunities are now equally available to all Americans, regardless of skin color.

We have even had a two-term black president, a once unthinkable proposition in this country.

Yet, the progress we have made has not led us anywhere closer to the much-touted post-racial America. The hope that the stain of Jim Crow would have washed away and Americans of all stripes would be living with one another in racial harmony seems even more fantastical today than in Martin Luther King's era. The election of Barack Obama to the presidency was considered a milestone in America's racial progress, and it was thought that race relations would dramatically improve after this momentous event. Just the opposite occurred, however. In the final year of President Obama's time in office, 69 percent of Americans believed race relations were in a horrid state.[1] The multiple race riots that erupted in the 2010s played a role in that development. So did the polarizing reactions to high-profile police-involved shootings and the movement spawned by those controversies, Black Lives Matter.

Nowhere else is America's growing racial tension more apparent than at your stereotypical college campus. Most of the disturbances, particularly the demonstrations at Yale University and the University of Missouri, have centered on race.

The typical tale of a college controversy goes something like this: An incident, or more likely an *alleged* incident, occurs that strikes minority students as racist. Protests break out and demands are sent to administrators to rectify the problem. Administrators flail helplessly around as they issue statements sympathetic to the cause of the offended. Then the agitators up the ante by claiming the school is filled with racism and white supremacy. After that, the school caves in to some of the agitators' demands, and the outrage eventually ebbs away.

Whether a school makes a major change or not—whether by renaming a building or letting a problematic administrator go— the culture of a college campus ensures this kind of behavior can occur on a regular basis. The mantra of white guilt lets campus activists feel that they are owed restitution for the oppression that is all around them.

Many years ago, America's race relations were shaped by white supremacy. Today, they are shaped by white guilt, a mind-set that in many ways resembles an inverted form of white supremacy. The Caucasian advocates for slavery and colonialism argued that the white man should rule over all the other races due to his superior values, intellect, martial skill, and other esteemed traits. White supremacy made light skin a marker of those qualities. All white people, as one whole collective, could claim this higher status due to their racial identity.

White guilt flips this script. Instead of white skin serving as a marker for superior values, it's a sign of inheriting a multitude of past injustices. No matter your actions, background, or beliefs, you carry the burden of European oppression if you are white. If your ancestors were struggling to get by in Poland during the Civil War, you still carry the taint of slavery. If your parents marched with Martin Luther King, you still retain the shame of segregation. If you do everything you can to call out the racism of your friends, you still bear the responsibility for colonialism.

To give it a clear definition, white guilt is the collective shame all white people must share for the past crimes of a few long-dead Caucasians against other groups. This is the new white man's burden.

The basis for white guilt is acceptance of the premise of left-wing intellectual Susan Sontag: "The white race is the cancer of human history."[2] Upon accepting that notion (or at least a far less brutal articulation of it), whites must strive for atonement from all the groups they have wronged. The feeling of superiority driven in by white supremacy is replaced with a state of utter shame under white guilt. The only kind of racial discussion whites should engage in are ones where they sit down, shut up, and allow their moral superiors to berate them.

A critical and succinct summary of the white guilt mantra was best captured by the 1980s hardcore punk band Minor Threat in their song "Guilty of Being White": The song is a lament by the singer, Ian MacKaye, that he is blamed for a lynching he had nothing to do with and a slavery that took place a century before he was born—all because he is white.

And this was an anthem penned by an avowed left-wing antiracist.

The new racial hierarchy fits perfectly with a victimhood moral culture. Whites practiced dominance in the past and still have privilege in our time. Thus, they are bad. Nonwhites, particularly African-Americans, were the victims of this dominance, and, by dint of oppression, are good. In the same manner, only whites can be racist, while nonwhites cannot be due to who historically controlled power in Western societies.

A preeminent example of white guilt playing itself out on a college campus is Georgetown University's proposed atonement for slavery. The elite D.C. school decided at the start of its fall 2016 semester to made amends for the Jesuit heads of the institution selling slaves way back in 1838. The primary method for Georgetown's penance is giving preferential admissions treatment to the descendants of those slaves—basically an expanded affirmative action for African-Americans.

Buildings named after the university presidents involved in the slave sale were renamed, a new institute to study slavery was established, more investment in diversity was announced, a walking tour to guilt-trip new students about slavery was incorporated into freshman programming, and the school promised to look into mandating "sensitivity training" to better Georgetown's "racial climate."[3] The Jesuit-run school topped it off with a Mass of Reconciliation, begging for forgiveness for the actions of men who passed away in the 1800s.

"We live today with the legacy of the failure to ameliorate the original evil of slavery in America," Georgetown University president John DeGioia said of his institute's plan. "We need all of our institutions, but especially our universities, which are among the most stable and enduring institutions that we have, to accept responsibility right now. Unless we're able to reconcile ourselves to that history and ensure that we have a framework for full equity of all of our people, we will not be able to progress as a nation."[4]

The view that whites should, as a collective, feel bad for being white can be found in the pages of America's papers of record and its best sellers. A fine representation of white guilt doctrine comes from a *New York Times* op-ed published, strangely, on Christmas Eve 2015. The *Times* gave Emory University professor George Yancy, a specialist in "Critical Whiteness Studies," an opportunity to address all of white America in a letter styled, appropriately, "Dear White America."

Yancy's message to his fellow light-skinned citizens was simple: you all are racist.

"If you are white and you are reading this letter, I ask that you don't run to seek shelter from your racism," the African-American professor argued with great confidence. "Being neither a 'good' white person nor a liberal white person will get you off the proverbial hook."

The reason why all whites are racist is because nonwhites have to live under the "yoke of whiteness" in American society. "As you reap comfort from being white, we suffer for being black and people of color," Yancy said. While placing all this guilt upon his white readers, the whiteness expert says that what he is really offering Caucasians is a gift of "love." That gift is the apparent understanding that you must wage an unyielding war against "yourself, your white identity, your white power, your white privilege."[5]

White guilt doctrine seeps through every pore of Yancy's letter, complete with the declaration that racism is a symptom of white birth and the call for all Caucasians to cleanse themselves of their foul whiteness. Yancy was not presenting a particularly original view in his column. In fact, it was very derivative—down to its overbearing, overwritten prose—of essayist Ta-Nehisi Coates's work.

Coates's chart-topping *Between the World and Me* spent multiple weeks on best-seller lists and was described by one prominent critic as "essential, like water or air."[6] While not quite as effusive as that comment, reviewers in every major outlet heaped unprecedented amounts of praise on Coates and lashed out at anyone who dared to criticize his writing.[7] Written as a letter to his son, *Between the World and Me* presents America as a place where "black bodies" are threatened and violated every day. The nation's culture is hardwired to prolong the destruction of black bodies, according to Coates's worldview. Everything about America for blacks is dour in *Between the World and Me*, as its author makes sure to pack every page with painful imagery of oppression and violence. To Coates, white supremacy is inherent in this country's nature, and he is doubtful America will ever root out the cancer.

This dread of the country he was born into leads him to have an ambivalent attitude toward the tragedies that have befallen the United States, such as the September 11 terror attacks. "I would never consider any American citizen pure," he said, recalling what he felt on the day the twin towers fell. "I was out of sync with the city. I kept thinking about how southern Manhattan had always been Ground Zero for us. They auctioned our bodies down there, in that same devastated, and rightly named, financial district. And there was once a burial ground for the auctioned there."

Then he turned his attention to the police officers and firefighters who lost their lives that day, charging into the towers to rescue their fellow citizens. Coates couldn't distinguish them from the police officer who shot and killed his friend, Prince Jones. "They were not human to me," he wrote of the 9/11 first responders. "Black, white, or whatever, they were the menaces of nature; they were the fire, the comet, the storm, which could— with no justification—shatter my body."[8]

The lesson to his son appears to be one of nihilistic paranoia. Police will murder you. Banks will deny you a mortgage. The media denies your black beauty. Coates does not offer any real hope for changing this grim reality. To a black reader, his words are an incitement to despise America and the whites who supposedly control it. It's natural for Black Lives Matter (BLM) to employ the same rhetoric as Coates to denounce America as a white supremacist creation and share the same jarring fixation with calling minorities "black and brown bodies."

It is a remarkable feat that a white supremacist society would confer so many honors upon a man who condemns it so strongly. Besides earning praise from every major publication, *Between the World and Me* won the 2015 National Book Award and was a finalist for the Pulitzer Prize. Coates got invited to speak at the very prestigious Aspen Ideas Festival, giving him the chance to rub elbows with some of the world's most powerful people. At least one college, the Washington University at St. Louis, made his book required reading for all incoming freshmen in 2016.[9] For someone who thinks a system is out to destroy his body, Coates seems awfully embedded into the establishment. While he claims he doesn't write for white people, many of his biggest fans are of a pasty extraction.[10] To white liberals, the black writer's word is gospel, and his imprecations against the past sins of whites are catnip to their guilt-laden consciences. They have no qualms about the Manichean narrative Coates weaves of noble, innocent blacks suffering constantly at the hands of malicious, immoral whites. And they seem to have no problem with the best-selling author exploiting their guilt to argue for whites to give reparations to blacks.

Before publication of his best seller, the acclaimed essayist was most famous for making the case for reparations in the pages of the *Atlantic*. Just as he did later in his book, Coates outlined in his 2014 essay a dark picture of America's racial history, one filled with murder, torture, enslavement, isolation, enforced poverty, and perpetual injustice against blacks.[11]

"America begins in black plunder and white democracy, two features that are not contradictory but complementary," Coates declared in the middle of his catalog of crimes and terrors indicting whites for their treatment of African-Americans. Those injustices range from denying home ownership to blacks in nice neighborhoods to brutal lynchings occurring in the early years of the twentieth century. All of them add up to a fifteen-thousand-word verdict that America was founded on white supremacy:

> To ignore the fact that one of the oldest republics in the world was erected on a foundation of white supremacy, to pretend that the problems of a dual society are the same as the problems of unregulated capitalism, is to cover the sin of national plunder with the sin of national lying. The lie ignores the fact that reducing American poverty and ending white supremacy are not the same. The lie ignores the fact that closing the "achievement gap" will do nothing to close the "injury gap," in which black college graduates still suffer higher unemployment rates than white college graduates, and black job applicants without criminal records enjoy roughly the same chance of getting hired as white applicants with criminal records.[12]

He defends his long litany against American history as an absolute necessity to shake whites from their refusal to acknowledge the country was built on racial prejudice. To accept that argument, one must accept the desideratum for reparations:

> Black history does not flatter American democracy; it chastens it. The popular mocking of reparations as a harebrained scheme

authored by wild-eyed lefties and intellectually unserious black nationalists is fear masquerading as laughter. Black nationalists have always perceived something unmentionable about America that integrationists dare not acknowledge—that white supremacy is not merely the work of hotheaded demagogues, or a matter of false consciousness, but a force so fundamental to America that it is difficult to imagine the country without it.[13]

To conservatives who preach personal responsibility and restoring the family, instead of reparations, as the cures for the ills of the black community, Coates shoots back, "The laments about 'black pathology,' the criticism of black family structures by pundits and intellectuals, ring hollow in a country whose existence was predicated on the torture of black fathers, on the rape of black mothers, on the sale of black children. An honest assessment of America's relationship to the black family reveals the country to be not its nurturer but its destroyer."

The writer does not offer any concrete plans for what reparations would amount to—just an endorsement that we, as a country, need to look into the matter. We'll figure out the specifics later. Right now, reparations are an ideal, as emancipation was for abolitionists before Abraham Lincoln moved into the White House, Coates asserts. He wants his writing to serve as the tinder for the dreams of the activists today who will make it a reality tomorrow.

Yet it's not clear if whites acknowledging the specter of white supremacy and agreeing to atone will do anything to ameliorate race relations. Instead, it could incentivize blacks and other minorities to keep demanding more from the guilty party. Shortly after Georgetown announced it was going to seek forgiveness for its role in slavery, those slave descendants who were set to receive special admissions preference and other amenities felt all that wasn't good enough. They wanted a *billion*-dollar "foundation for reconciliation" on top of all the other amends.[14]

If whites submit to their guilt and beg for penance from the races they have wronged, there's no limit to what the morally superior groups will extract from the now-capitulated oppressor. Especially when that unequal relationship gives them power to make extraordinary demands. The admission of guilt only serves to intensify the grievances of those who feel whites have done them wrong.

Coates positively cited black nationalists in his case for reparations, but he is certainly not an adherent to that ideology. He does not hope for a separate state for blacks—he just wants reparations and for whites to inculcate the guilt that's imparted by his view of history. It's not black supremacy either, as he does not argue for blacks to rule over whites or propound on all the better attributes that blacks have over whites. Instead, Coates's ideas fit nicely into the victimhood culture where whites are presented as morally inferior due to their privilege, and blacks are morally superior due to their oppression. The implied agenda is not about the traditional power structure associated with a term such as *black supremacy*; it's centered on a moral hierarchy. Coates also does not believe in race as a biologically fixed concept, as many black nationalists do. Race is a social construct, according to him, and his primary hope is that we one day eliminate all racial categories.

Yet, being a writer focused exclusively on race and wanting one artificially constructed group to hand over unspecific restitution to another artificially constructed group undermines that whole "do away with race" hope. America's current racial discourse, as exemplified by Coates, only solidifies racialism dominating our society. Assigning guilt to one entire group for the past sins of a few men with "whiteness" keeps race alive and well. This rhetoric also offers lots of sweet rewards for those who engage it, like Mr. Coates. Thanks to his work on oppression, he's now able to afford a swanky, $2 million brownstone in New York City.[15]

To keep up the effort to inculcate white guilt, BLM activists, professors, and others are very fond of using two terms for portraying America as a racist country: "white privilege" and "systemic racism."

White privilege refers to the inherent societal benefits Caucasians receive merely by living in America and other Western countries. That racial privilege is exclusive to whites as a group and is completely unearned, according to those who buy into the concept. A term that was once mainly reserved for academic and left-wing circles just a few years ago, "white privilege" has now gone mainstream. It even made appearances on the 2016 campaign trail, with Hillary Clinton acknowledging that she and other whites do in fact benefit from white privilege.[16]

But what does having white privilege even mean? The explanation most widely used in education circles comes from the 1980s. Self-described antiracism activist and Wellesley College professor Peggy McIntosh wrote an essay, "White Privilege: Unpacking the Invisible Knapsack," that detailed how white privilege supposedly works and the hypothetical situations where Caucasians have an edge over minorities. She wrote:

I think whites are carefully taught not to recognize white privilege, as males are taught not to recognize male privilege. So I have begun in an untutored way to ask what it is like to have white privilege. I have come to see white privilege as an invisible package of unearned assets that I can count on cashing in each day, but about which I was 'meant' to remain oblivious. White privilege is like an invisible weightless knapsack of special provisions, maps, passports, codebooks, visas, clothes, tools, and blank checks.

The main part of her essay lists fifty advantages she has in life that her "African-American coworkers, friends, and acquaintances" can't enjoy. Among them: "If I want to, I can be pretty sure of finding a publisher for this piece on white privilege"; "I can be casual about whether or not to listen to another person's voice in a group in which s/he is the only member of his/her race"; "I can go into a music shop and count on finding the music of my race represented, into a supermarket and find the staple foods which fit with my cultural traditions, into a hairdresser's shop and find someone who can cut my hair"; "I do not have to educate my children to be aware of systemic racism for their own daily physical protection"; and "I can talk with my mouth full and not have people put this down to my color."[17]

The main gist of McIntosh's argument is that social norms and habits are inherently discriminatory to African-Americans and other minorities. A day at the supermarket is no big deal for whites, according to the activist injustice. For nonwhites, it's a struggle that comes with a cart full of risks. This standard isn't due to government mandate or individual acts of meanness, but to the way our social system is structured for the supposed benefit of light-skinned Americans. McIntosh concludes that white privilege amounts to unearned power that allows Caucasians to escape to comfort and dominate other groups. The success of whites is not well earned—it comes from an unjust system that punishes other races. Thus, individual whites should not be so quick to tout their achievements when they are ill gotten, according to white privilege theory.

The theory of white privilege reasons that individual whites do well in America not solely due to hard work, as the unjust system puts fewer impediments in their way to success. It's a rather stark rebuke to the traditional American values of individualism and personal responsibility. Your success is not due to your busting your ass to get where you are; it's a result of an unjust system that favors people who look like you.

Whites are supposed to follow the lead of Hillary Clinton and others and feel bad and "check" their privilege. "Check your privilege!" has become both a rally cry and a favorite insult among campus agitators, as it forces their opponents to demonstrate moral inferiority before the aggrieved youth. At the end of her essay, McIntosh urged whites to accept their unearned power and use it for the benefit of the oppressed races around them by "reconstruct[ing] power systems on a broader base."

White privilege is essentially a concept for explaining how a nation that no longer tolerates institutional racism still discriminates against nonwhites. It fits with the general idea that this nation still suffers from "systemic racism." For a term that is so frequently used, it's tough to find a concise definition of it, and activists seem to utilize it to describe multiple phenomena. Often the term is used interchangeably with the phrases "institutional racism" and "structural racism."

The Aspen Institute, which has hosted Ta-Nehisi Coates

numerous times, argued that systemic racism is synonymous with its preferred term, structural racism. The highly esteemed nonprofit defined structural racism as

> a system in which public policies, institutional practices, cultural representations, and other norms work in various, often reinforcing ways to perpetuate racial group inequity. It identifies dimensions of our history and culture that have allowed privileges associated with "whiteness" and disadvantages associated with "color" to endure and adapt over time. Structural racism is not something that a few people or institutions choose to practice. Instead it has been a feature of the social, economic and political systems in which we all exist.

This form of discrimination is different from institutional racism, according to the Institute. "Institutional racism refers to the policies and practices within and across institutions that, intentionally or not, produce outcomes that chronically favor, or put a racial group at a disadvantage," its guideline explains. "Poignant examples of institutional racism can be found in school disciplinary policies in which students of color are punished at much higher rates that their white counterparts, in the criminal justice system, and within many employment sectors in which day-to-day operations, as well as hiring and firing practices can significantly disadvantage workers of color."[18]

Whatever differences might exist between these terms, the one most used by activists and pundits to advocate for Black Lives Matter is *systemic racism*. The way it's deployed often covers both definitions of structural and institutional racism. Systemic racism explains why African-Americans are incarcerated disproportionately (rather than because they commit more crime per capita than other groups)[19] and why the descendants of slaves are not as economically successful as whites. It's because we live in a system that's white supremacist to its core, even with a black president, a black U.S. attorney general, and hundreds of black judges. Systemic racism places the problems of blacks onto the shoulders of whites and negates the agency of African-Americans to improve their lot. "You cannot truly succeed in a white supremacist nation when you're black" is the intended message of this rhetoric.

The incessant harping on white privilege and systemic racism justifies grievance mongering and downplays the power an individual has over his own life. Whatever is wrong in a campus activist's life can be blamed on the invisible white supremacy of the system, thereby giving him or her carte blanche to feel righteously aggrieved while never having to cast a skeptical eye inward. When activists cite systemic racism, they are saying the American system is made to put blacks and other minorities at a disadvantage. That's why there is so much energy for issuing extreme demands to college administrators to eliminate their own version of systemic racism.

And many times, those demands can come off as downright loopy.

The demands of black activists present a stark, racially cen-tered focus and are issued with the hope of giving additional advantages to students based on their skin color. Before Black Lives Matter's national emergence, a group calling itself By Any Means Necessary staged a sit-in at the University of Michigan in April 2014 to demand the admission of unqualified black students. The demonstrators argued that a drop in academic requirements exclusively for blacks was needed to increase minority enrollment. To not do so was an injustice.[20] The Black Student Union, an ally of By Any Means Necessary, had threatened "physical action" a few months earlier if Michigan did not build a $300,000 multicultural facility, among other demands. The school caved in on that costly item.[21]

The 2014 police-involved shooting death of Michael Brown in Ferguson, Missouri, ignited the Black Lives Matter movement, and soon similar protests became a regular feature at college campuses. The fall 2015 semester saw these campus-based protests for "racial justice" reach a new height of absurdity, with exorbitant demands issued in response to every microaggression witnessed. The most famous instance of this kind of agitation occurred at the University of Missouri in November of that year. A series of small, unrelated incidents at the campus riled up a core group of agitators to claim their school was infested with racism. The incidents that so angered these students include the African-American student body president claiming he was called the n-word by mysterious men in a truck, the discovery of a swastika drawn in fecal matter in a dorm bathroom, and a protest leader alleging the university president's car hit him during a parade. (Video footage revealed the lead agitator was at most tapped by the vehicle after running in front of it.)[22]

That car-assaulted protest leader, Jonathan Butler, later started a hunger strike to protest Mizzou's bigotry. Thirty-two black MU football players, in an act of solidarity with Butler, vowed to boycott any of their team's remaining games if the protester's demands were not met,[23] the chief demand being the resignation of the university's president, Tim Wolfe, for his failure to adequately address Mizzou's systemic racism. Besides being falsely accused of hitting Butler with a car, Wolfe was disliked for his failure a few days before the football strike to give the desired answer to irate students when asked what systematic oppression is. He quickly resigned after the announcement of the footballers' boycott, but did not apologize for his "white male privilege" as the campus agitators—organized under the name Concerned Student 1950—requested. After their triumph, Mizzou's social justice warriors got nuttier under the strain of national attention in making threats against journalists and conjuring up wild claims of Klansmen running loose on campus.

They also did not stop advocating for their other demands, which included specific racial quotas for black students and faculty (an unconstitutional request, according to the Supreme Court), mandatory "racial awareness" curriculum, and special counseling exclusively for minority students.[24]

The special academic help Mizzou's racial activists desired appears to be a result of the mismatch theory in action. The students struggle academically because they got into a school that was beyond their skill level thanks to racial preferences in college admissions. Instead of blaming a system that judges them by their skin color, or their own failures to study, they blame the invisible systemic racism of the schools they attend for why their grades aren't so great.

During the same semester, protesters at numerous other schools issued similar demands in response to offensive campus incidents. A group calling itself the "Afrikan Student Union" at the University of California–Los Angeles released extensive demands in the wake of a fraternity hosting a hip-hop-themed party. ASU declared the school must impose expanded racial quotas in admissions and hiring, create a $30 million endowment for the sole purpose of financially supporting black students, and erect cheaper off-campus housing exclusively for African-Americans.[25] In response, the school announced a plan to "develop more robust anti-discrimination policies" and hire outreach officers to increase black recruitment to UCLA. Those plans disappointed ASU, and the group stuck to their initial demands.[26]

However, the nearby California State University–Los Angeles caved in to their activists' radical demands at the start of the fall 2016 semester by offering African-American students black-only dormitories to protect them from microaggressions. The reason for the segregated living areas is to "provide a cheaper alternative housing solution for Black students. This space would also serve as a safe space for Black CSLA students to congregate, connect, and learn from each other," according to the racial activists desiring the return of Jim Crow.[27]

A recent graduate at the University of Kansas initiated his own hunger strike in support of the campus's radical group "Rock Chalk Invisible Hawk" shortly after Mizzou's eruption. The group demanded the school impose racial awareness workshops for all students, enroll more illegal immigrants, and spend more on multicultural affairs. The agitation came as a result of an unsubstantiated allegation that a gun was pulled on black students at a house party.[28] Agitators at the University of North Carolina–Chapel Hill disrupted a late November town hall hosted by the school to issue their race-based demands. It featured the usual topics of increased racial quotas and more spending on diversity, along with calls for gender-neutral bathrooms and salaries for student-athletes.[29]

All told, nearly eighty universities witnessed this kind of demand activism during the 2015–16 school year, according to the Black Liberation Collective,[30] a group set up to coordinate efforts between these radical outbursts. BLC issued its own demands for students nationwide to advocate for:

1. WE DEMAND at the minimum, Black students and Black faculty to be reflected by the national percentage of Black folk in the state and the country

2. WE DEMAND free tuition for Black and indigenous students

3. WE DEMAND a divestment from prisons and an investment in communities[31]

BLC's stated principles echo the thought of Ta-Nehisi Coates—with accusations that white supremacy is fundamental to America's founding and blacks are thoroughly dehumanized by our society—along with bromides against sexism, homophobia, and ableism. The group also condones violence to achieve its goals. "We will strive for liberation by any means necessary, including but not limited to: armed self-defense. We condone whatever methods Black people adopt to liberate themselves and their kin," its statement of principles declares.[32]

These groups' beliefs and demands reveal an explicit racial intent. The benefits desired are only for black students, and it appears these agitators hope to make African-Americans a privileged caste at all universities. The chief rhetorical tools for achieving this vision are accusations of systemic racism, a great play on the intense white guilt of campus administrators and student leaders. While blacks are exulted as noble victims, whites, the perceived oppressors, are seen in a hateful light.

Antiwhite attitudes are evidenced by the infamous Dartmouth University library rampage where African-Americans physically attacked white students (which earned an apology from the administration . . . to the assaulters),[33] and Mizzou demonstrators segregated "white allies" away from everybody else.[34] White hatred manifests itself in actual crimes committed by black students against their Caucasian peers. "That's for 400 years of slavery, you bitch," disgraced Vanderbilt University football player Corey Batey told the unconscious white victim of a notorious gang rape he participated in with other teammates, all of whom except for one were black. Batey delivered that message while urinating on the victim.[35]

Maybe these bigoted souls are just following the example set by the universities they attend, as several schools have launched initiatives that can only be interpreted as antiwhite. One of the more popular forms of discrimination against whites is to have Caucasian-only antiracist training. The University of Wisconsin–Madison unveiled its own version of this training in the spring of 2016. The Big Ten school created "The Privilege of Whiteness" workshops, which are intended to shame Caucasians for their whiteness and are "designed for a White audience." During the same semester, Oregon State University hosted segregated social justice retreats where white students were taught to check their privilege, while nonwhites were encouraged to be empowered. The University of Vermont and Northwestern University held similar white-only social justice retreats during the 2015–16 school year where the mission was to make Caucasians feel bad for their skin color.[36]

Other schools have found different avenues for making their campuses less friendly to whites.

In recent years, Western Washington University has dedicated itself to making its campus less white. "Every year, from this stage and at this time, you have heard me say that, if in decades ahead, we are as white as we are today, we will have failed as university," WWU president Bruce Shepard said in a 2012 address. The school showed its commitment to this goal by distributing a questionnaire to all students and faculty in 2014 asking, "How do we make sure that in future years 'we are not as white as we are today?'"[37]

Apparently, that mission had not been achieved, as WWU students issued radical demands in 2016 to dismantle the "white supremacist" structures at the college. Those demands included the creation of a "College of Power and Liberation," enacting a task force designed to closely monitor the speech of students, and building racially segregated residence halls.[38]

The State University of New York at Binghamton included as a part of its 2016 training for resident assistants a program called #StopWhitePeopl2k16. "The premise of this session is to help others take the next step in understanding diversity, privilege, and the society we function within," the class description explained. "Learning about these topics is a good first step, but when encountered with 'good' arguments from uneducated people, how do you respond? This open discussion will give attendees the tools to do so, and hopefully expand upon what they may already know." The point of the session was to learn how to verbally overcome those who may not buy into white privilege and drill it into their heads.[39] This school-sanctioned event put on at taxpayers' expense was supported by the school's student affairs, before administrators apologized for its title. Binghamton officials still claimed that the session was not antiwhite, however, after delivering an apology.[40]

As students arrived for the fall 2016 semester at California's Pomona College, they were greeted with posters advising them on how to be better white allies. The three steps to making a good white ally included: "1. Be prepared to make mistakes. 2. Listen and apologize. 3. Make sure to change." It then let white students know that they are all racist. "Understand that you are white, so it is inevitable that you have unconsciously learned racism," the poster stated. "Your unearned advantage must be acknowledged and your racism unlearned."[41] The notices follow Pomona hosting multiple events that excluded white people from participating in them during the previous academic year.[42]

The actions of Mizzou students and other protesters brought a massive backlash against their racial activism, but it does not appear the radical zeitgeist will disappear anytime soon. The University of Missouri's 2016 freshman orientation featured a program where the protesters of the previous year were celebrated as civil rights heroes, showing that not everyone views their actions with dismay.[43]

The toxic racial climate of colleges looks to be perpetuated into the upcoming years as white guilt remains established as an unchallenged dogma. Hate against white-skinned students can only increase in ferocity when nonwhites are told to blame their failures in life on white supremacy and are taught to see Western history as one long tale of domination and violence against people of color. Those messages don't result in love for the modern descendants of those white devils. On the flip side, when white students are inundated with these diatribes against them, there's a good chance many will reject what they are taught and say they are tired of the guilt trips.

Whether that backlash will make our campuses less tumultuous, or just lead to more hostility between students, is anyone's guess.

6

RAPE CULTURE FEMINISM

"For 1 in 5 women, their dream school will be their nightmare."

That was the tagline for the much-touted 2015 documentary *The Hunting Ground*. The film covered the widely discussed sexual assault epidemic on college campuses. Most studies on the matter purport to show that one in five females are at risk of being sexually assaulted at some point during their college career. The poster on which the film's tagline found itself emblazoned resembles the famous promotional pictures for *The Exorcist*, hinting that the innocent girl walking up those dark stairs at night is heading toward her doom.

The horror movie imagery and tagline are not-so-subtle cues telling potential viewers that something terrifying is happening to young women across the country. It remains nameless in the promotion, but the notion that college girls are being dragged away and violently raped on a regular basis is planted in the minds of those who see the poster. Why else does the faceless woman look as if she's climbing up the *Exorcist* stairs, surrounded by the creepiest campus locale imaginable?

The problem is, that notion—much like *The Hunting Ground*—is not at all accurate. Nonetheless, the "1 in 5" figure from this documentary has become an article of faith among the campus Left, and "rape culture" has become the defining focus of college-based feminism.

What is feminism in the second decade of the twenty-first century? It's complicated. Feminism, as a philosophy, is now commonly bracketed out into three different waves. First-wave feminism lasted until the first half of the twentieth century and was concerned primarily with securing the right to vote and other basic civil rights for women. Second-wave feminism dominated in the 1960s and '70s, and its primary advocacy goal was ensuring workplace equality for women. Third-wave feminism first emerged in the 1980s and is now the predominant ideological focus of the movement. Unlike its predecessors, its goals and concerns are not as clear-cut.

The prevalent stated goal of third-wave feminism is to advocate for more diversity and celebrate the differences among women. Thinking that past iterations were too white and too privileged, the third wave tries to highlight how the new struggle includes people of color and other disadvantaged groups. It also stresses diversity of attitudes toward such topics as sex and dress. You don't have to declare yourself a man-hating, short-haired "womyn" anymore to be a true feminist. That's one of the few, if not the only, positive developments of third-wave feminism over its precursors.

While the goals of the new feminism are not as obvious as those of the previous waves, they do have their problems they'd like to fix. The difference is that the issues they harp on are not the effects of institutional discrimination or faulty laws. Rather, they are social habits and trends that, in all likelihood, cannot be rectified by legislation.

Some of the very important issues modern feminists fret about include mansplaining (alleged condescending explanations given by men to women), manspreading (men hogging too much space on public transportation), and catcalling (men shouting unsolicited compliments in public spaces). Feminist websites such as Jezebel and Wonkette offer up a daily tally of outrages on the oh-so-pressing level as manspreading. It's hard to overlook the impression that third-wave feminism is a vehicle for transforming petty annoyances into injustices on the scale of ethnic cleansing.

The issues feminists find important may seem, for the most part, completely frivolous. However, their one problem that has the power to shock the average person is college rape culture. Rape is one of the worst crimes a man can commit. It permanently traumatizes the victim and forever tarnishes her peace of mind. To men, it represents a grave crime against a weaker person and violates the victim's sense of honor. It is little wonder that those convicted of sex crimes suffer the most violence and harassment in our prison system.[1] In the average person's mind, rape comes second only to murder on the crime hierarchy. That's why the assumption that it's happening to thousands of young women is so powerful—and such an effective argument for feminist goals. The media, fortunately for feminists, have bought hook, line, and sinker into rape hysteria.

Numerous headlines in recent years have screamed that there's a campus rape epidemic:

"Study Finds 'Epidemic Level' of Rape on College Campus"[2]

"Undeniably Massive Study Confirms Campus Rape Is an Undeniable, Massive Problem"[3]

"U.S. Bureau of Justice Statistics' Campus Climate Study Confirms Epidemic of College Sexual Assault"[4]

"How 'The Hunting Ground' Uncovers the Campus Rape Epidemic"[5]

These are just a few examples of the rhetoric surrounding this supposed crisis. Multiple groups are dedicated to eradicating the menace, one of which calls itself simply enough EROC, short for "End Rape on Campus." The alleged campus rape epidemic is fomented by what the believers see as an insidious rape culture rooted in campus life.

What exactly constitutes a rape culture? According to Emilie Buchwald, who helped write a book on the subject, a rape culture is:

a complex set of beliefs that encourage male sexual aggression and support violence against women. It is a society where violence is seen as sexy and sexuality as violent. In a rape culture, women perceive a continuum of threatened violence that ranges from sexual remarks to sexual touching to rape itself. A rape culture condones physical and emotional terrorism against women as the norm . . . In a rape culture both men and women assume that sexual violence is a fact of life, inevitable . . . However . . . much of what we accept as inevitable is in fact the expression of values and attitudes that can change.[6]

Rape culture, in the eyes its believers, permeates every part of the society it infects. As explained by the website Force: Upsetting the Rape Culture:

Rape culture includes jokes, TV, music, advertising, legal jargon, laws, words and imagery, that make violence against women and sexual coercion seem so normal that people believe that rape is inevitable. Rather than viewing the culture of rape as a problem to change, people in a rape culture think about the persistence of rape as "just the way things are."

Both of these viewpoints are considered so poignant that the advocacy group Women against Violence against Women highlighted them in their section on rape culture.[7]

Colleges are seen as the quintessential example of this insidious phenomenon in action due to the studies showing the high victimization rate and the perception by feminists that it's a huge problem. *Bustle*, a blog geared for millennial women, offered four reasons why colleges perpetuate a rape culture: (1) the "Fraternity Culture" of colleges; (2) the "Drinking Culture" that exists at most colleges; (3) "'No Means No' Consent Education" (because it fails to "clarify that only an enthusiastic 'yes' constitutes consent); and (4) the "Valorization of Student Athletes."[8] All of these elements serve to fortify male power over young women, diminish the boundaries of acceptable behavior, and normalize coercion, according to the author. A few are actually at fault for the rise in sexual assault claims and the perception that schools are ignoring the issue. A majority of cases alleging sexual assault involve alcohol clouding the judgment of consent for both parties involved. There's a multitude of examples of schools covering up rapes by star athletes.[9]

But it doesn't necessarily explain why there's a dreadful feeling that thousands of women are raped every year at their dream schools. All the outrage and protests over campus rape culture ultimately stem from the idea, backed up by studies, that one in five women (or one in four, as sometimes reported) are sexually assaulted at American colleges. That one figure drives the sentiment that coeds are at high risk for one of the worst imaginable crimes.

Except, one in five college women aren't actually at risk of sexual assault. The studies cited in support of the theory come with myriad issues that undermine the vaunted figure. The much-touted stat originally came from the 2007 National Institute of Justice Campus Sexual Assault (CSA) study.[10] A two-year long survey of two large public universities—one in the South and one in the Midwest—found that one in five of the female respondents had said they experienced what amounted to a sexual assault at some point in college. The findings were shocking to many, and provided the impetus for the Obama administration to issue draconian guidelines for tackling campus sexual violence and harassment. (More on that later.)

There's one issue, though, with the groundbreaking study: the researchers who oversaw it think it's wrong to apply on a national scale. "We feel we need to set the record straight," social scientists Christopher Krebs and Christine Lindquist wrote in a 2014 *Time* magazine op-ed on their famous study. "Although we used the best methodology available to us at the time, there are caveats that make it inappropriate to use the 1-in-5 number in the way it's being used today, as a baseline or the only statistic when discussing our country's problem with rape and sexual assault on campus."

Krebs and Lindquist made this assertion due to the limitations of their study. "The 1-in-5 statistic is not a nationally representative estimate of the prevalence of sexual assault, and we have never presented it as being representative of anything other than the population of senior undergraduate women at the two universities where data were collected," they stated.

Another major issue with the study is the acts it includes under the umbrella of sexual assault. Rape (unwanted sexual penetration) is only one of the acts assessed by the study. Also included within the sexual assault category are forced kissing and unwanted groping—both of which are common among heavily inebriated college students who lack the maturity to control themselves. While the authors stressed that those actions can be considered crimes under the law, they do not meet the commonly recognized criteria of what makes for a "sexual assault."

Another issue is that the surveyors had a very low response rate for their online questionnaire, which could have made the stats for sexual assault much higher. There was even a caveat in the research that could convince rape culture believers to stop relying on it: its one-in-five stat did not include those who reported attempted sexual assaults.

The CSA survey may not offer the best insight into the actual rate of campus sexual assault. But the figure it provided has become entrenched among feminists, and it appears every study that came after it has tried its hardest to prove the truth of the sacred number.

An example of one of these misleading studies is a survey published by the *Washington Post* in June 2015. "One in Five Women Say They Were Violated," was the article's headline, immediately reinforcing the standard campus sexual assault figure.[11] Conducted along with the Kaiser Family Foundation, the poll surveyed more than one thousand young adults who had attended college in the last four years and miraculously came out with a figure right under 20 percent. But like the CSA study, this poll had several issues.

Similar to the original study, the *Post's* survey included forced kissing and unwanted groping in its definition of sexual assault. The groping category included the odd act of involuntary "grinding," a sexualized dance prevalent at college parties. The survey didn't ask the students whether they felt these acts amounted to an assault—it just asked whether they had experienced the acts and lumped them all together under the broad term *sexual assault*. Apparently, the headline was assuming a bit by declaring that *every* one in five women felt violated.

A second problem with the study is how it treated "unwanted sexual contact" under the influence of alcohol or drugs. The *Daily Caller* News Foundation's Blake Neff pointed out that two-thirds of the respondents who claimed they'd had this kind of contact admitted to having been "unable to provide consent" at the time because they "were passed out, drugged, or drunk, incapacitated, or asleep." This kind of assault is markedly different from forced contact and is usually found to not meet the standards of assault in court. Even if an alleged victim is very drunk during the encounter, it may not serve as a credible accusation legally. Under the law, a victim must be so intoxicated by drugs or alcohol that she is either unconscious or otherwise unaware of what is taking place for it to qualify as an assault. The survey left this question murky as to whether the subjects who claimed violation after drunken sex met the legal requirement for rape.[12]

According to some of the anecdotes collected in *WaPo*'s article on the study, many of the women placed in the one in five did not have experiences that met the legal definition for incapacitated rape. One young lady said she couldn't recall if consent was granted, but remembered waking up from a drunken episode and feeling that something wrong had happened. But her alleged assaulter was also very drunk at the time of intercourse, and she told the paper, "It's like we're both raping each other." That's not actually rape though.

The *Post*'s poll was not alone in including muddled categories and dubiously worded questions in its findings. The CSA study also posed a similar question to its respondents on incapacitated rape that left it unclear if the students had actually given consent or considered it a legitimate assault. A 2010 Centers for Disease Control and Prevention report shared the same issue.[13]

With all these issues with its study, the *Post* still made the bold assertion—with virtually no evidence to back it—that the true number for sexual assaults is "probably even larger" than the "1 in 5" statistic. Maybe this claim was given in the *hope* that it's true rather than that it is actually true.

In fall 2015, the Association of American Universities (AAU) released its own study showing one in four college women run the risk of sexual assault. However, that figure comes with a host of caveats, which the authors make clear in the study's overview. "Estimates such as '1 in 5' or '1 in 4' as a global rate [are] oversimplistic, if not misleading. None of the studies which generate estimates for specific IHEs [institutes of higher education] are nationally representative," the introduction read. A major problem negating a national representation is the incredibly low response rate (19 percent) to the AAU's online survey. "An analysis of . . . non-response bias found estimates may be too high because non-victims may have been less likely to participate," the study states. And just like every other study previously mentioned, it included forced kissing and "sexual touching" in its parameters, as well as dubious questioning; and none of the questions posed to the respondents asked whether they felt they had been victims of a sexual assault.[14]

"It is ridiculous to suggest that American campuses, which all the data shows are some of the safest places for women, are hotbeds of rape with comparable sexual assault rates to war-torn African countries. It just doesn't pass the basic common sense test," British journalist Milo Yiannopoulos has astutely noted of the rape culture "moral panic" and its erroneous obsession with the one-in-five figure.[15]

While unrelated to the one-in-five tenet, another highly cited study used to further stoke campus rape hysteria is backed by questionable data as well. Acclaimed psychologist David Lisak authored a groundbreaking 2002 study on campus sexual assault that asserted the perpetrators of this crime are mostly serial offenders who are never brought to justice. This notion gives credence to the dark impression of campus sexual assault as one of violent rape and sinister men preying on helpless women without any concern of punishment. The Obama administration cited the Lisak study in a 2014 directive committed to eradicating the epidemic of college rape. However, *Reason* magazine cast significant doubt on this foundational study in 2015.

For one, Lisak never identified the four surveys, supposedly conducted in the 1990s, that he used to buttress his survey. In an interview with *Reason*, the researcher said it was probable that the findings were based on his doctoral research. The study itself was based on questionnaires passed out at a commuter school in Boston. The questionnaires were not primarily focused on sexual assault. The average age of the male respondents was 26.5—much older than the average college student. It is unclear whether the alleged repeat offenders were actually college students, if their victims were college students, or if the crimes took place on campus. The questionnaires also do not distinguish between an attacker striking multiple victims or assaulting the same person multiple times.[16]

Lisak has claimed he conducted thorough follow-up interviews with some of the serial rapists. However, his data appear mostly to come from anonymous interviews he conducted in the 1980s, not from the data collected in the 1990s from the Boston school. He refused to answer *Reason*'s questions requesting a clarification on the in-depth interrogations of serial predators. These issues have not stopped powerful people from hoisting the study as a sign of the horrors of campus rape and to justify believing outright lies, such as the University of Virginia gang rape hoax.[17]

The studies seem to all point to an incredibly high rate of victimization that is disturbingly on the rise. The official government data on the subject paint a very different picture. The Department of Justice's Bureau of Justice Statistics released an in-depth report on sexual assaults against college-aged women near the end of 2014.[18] The percentage of female college students who became victims of sexual assault was placed at 0.61 percent. To put that figure in the one-in-five way of thinking, that's 0.03 in 5—nowhere close to the article of faith. In addition to that revelation, the DOJ report found there was a higher rate of incidence among *non-college-attending* women than among their collegian peers. The study also found sexual assault had gone down from the late 1990s to the early 2010s. Both facts shed a skeptical light on the feeling that there's a rape epidemic ravaging higher education at the moment.[19]

Even for the colleges with the most reported cases of rape, the numbers don't even come close to the one-in-five number. Reed College, a small private arts institution in Oregon with the highest number of rape reports per capita according to the Department of Education, had a rape allegation of one per every seventy-eight students in 2014.[20] Assuming they were all allegations of male-on-female assaults and based on the female population of the school (54 percent[21]), the number comes out to roughly one in forty women at Reed College who alleged they were raped.

Stanford University, an apparent hotbed of campus rape due to the controversy surrounding the Stanford rape case of 2016, didn't even make the top ten list of schools with the highest rape allegations per capita, according to a *Washington Post* analysis of the data. It's worth remembering that these are rape reports, not rape convictions. So a number of the allegations included in DoE's data are likely either false or not considered rape by a court of law.

A close examination of all the studies show that the one-in-five figure is exaggerated at best. Young women seem to be facing an epidemic of bad dance moves, awkward dates, and poor decisions rather than a rash of violent rapes.

So why does everyone keep believing that college women are uniquely positioned to suffer an unimaginable crime? Simple: effective propaganda on the part of feminists and a media willing to take any lone story as an example of a broader crisis.

The Hunting Ground is a perfect example of this tactic. The film earned many accolades and has a very high, 93 percent critic score and an 83 percent audience score on the movie review aggregator Rotten Tomatoes.[22] One of the movie's most compelling elements is its highlight on specific cases that bring down the problem to the personal level. But in two of the cases the movie highlights were thrown out of court for lack of evidence and unreliable testimonies on the part of the alleged victims. The film gives a platform to notorious fabulist Emma "Mattress Girl" Sulkowicz, whose rape claim turned out to be illegitimate. The film also promotes the dubious one-in-five figure.[23] The facts were so out of line with *The Hunting Ground*'s narrative that a crew member took the desperate measure of editing *Wikipedia* articles to conform with the documentary's perspective.[24]

Considering its serious faults, the *Washington Examiner*'s Ashe Schow deduced that the movie "looks less like a documentary and more like a film in search of a problem."[25] *The Hunting Ground*'s many inaccuracies did not prevent CNN from broadcasting it to millions of Americans who would probably accept its premise without any further research.

In the summer of 2016, the media became fixated on the case of a Stanford University swimmer getting a slap on the wrist in court for raping an unconscious coed. The controversy was held up as an example of the horrific campus rape epidemic besetting our nation.[26] It also seemed to be the first time the media found a legitimate college rape to spew their outrage over.

Two years before the Stanford scandal, several media outlets were duped into believing two rape hoaxes. The first was the case of Emma Sulkowicz. Ms. Sulkowicz first gained attention after carrying a mattress around Columbia University to protest her alleged rapist remaining on campus. The act, which was part of a senior performance art project called "Carry Her Weight," attracted national attention and spurred other college women to haul mattresses around to protest campus sexual assault. For her efforts, Sulkowicz was invited by Sen. Kirsten Gillibrand (D-NY) to the 2015 State of the Union to highlight her cause.[27]

Despite all of her attention and honors, the Columbia coed's rape story was not accurate. The man she accused of assault, Paul Nungesser, later came out to give his side of the story—with the aid of multiple Facebook messages from his accuser. According to the evidence, the two had a consensual encounter that resulted in Sulkowicz desiring to see Nungesser more.[28] Her messages to him practically begged for more sex in very explicit terms. It appears the rape claim—which she waited eight months after their interaction to file—is a result of Nungesser not responding to those messages.

The more famous rape story of 2014 is the notorious *Rolling Stone* "A Rape on Campus" hoax. *Rolling Stone* published a lengthy report by Sabrina Rubin Erdely on a terrifying gang rape of a young University of Virginia freshman identified only as "Jackie" in the article (her real name was later revealed to be Jackie Coakley). Coakley told Erdely that she was brutally raped by seven members of a UVA fraternity as part of a pledge ritual. The "Rape on Campus" article went into graphic detail on the crime. After its publication, outrage reached peak level in the national media outlets. The house of the accused fraternity, Phi Kappa Psi, was vandalized and saw daily protests outside its doors. The university suspended all fraternities for the remainder of the semester.[29]

Eventually, Coakley's story unraveled. Turns out she never visited the fraternity house, was never assaulted, and made up the whole story as one part of an elaborate scheme to convince a reluctant friend to date her. *Rolling Stone* later retracted the story and the whole episode is now seen as a sobering example of journalistic malpractice.[30] Multiple lawsuits were filed against the magazine by the school, officials named in the article, and the wrongly accused fraternity.

The fixation on campus sexual violence is not entirely the work of feminist journalists. It was given a tremendous boost by the Obama administration during the president's tenure.

In April 2011, the Department of Education's Office of Civil Rights issued a "Dear Colleague" letter advancing new policies concerning sexual violence and sexual harassment within higher education. According to the letter, the "statistics on sexual violence are both deeply troubling and a call to action for the nation." The "call to action" proposed by the letter was applying Title IX law (which prohibits discrimination on the basis of sex in education) to require colleges to handle sexual assault and harassment allegations in a more diligent manner.[31]

The Foundation for Individual Rights in Education (FIRE), however, found the new standards mandated by the White House to be a catastrophe.

> With regard to due process, OCR's [Office of Civil Rights] April 4 letter requires colleges and universities investigating and hearing allegations of sexual harassment and sexual violence on campus to use a "preponderance of the evidence" standard to determine if someone is guilty. This standard merely requires that it is "more likely than not" that someone is responsible for what they are accused of, and it is our judiciary's lowest standard of proof. This is because whoever is serving as the "jury" in such a case need only be 50.01% certain that the accused person is at fault.
>
> Given the seriousness of allegations of sexual misconduct—which range from sexual harassment to rape—FIRE believes that requiring universities to find accused students guilty based on this "more likely than not" standard does not sufficiently protect the accused person's right to due process . . .
>
> In another threat to due process rights, OCR is mandating that if a university judicial process allows the accused student to appeal a verdict, it must also allow the accusing student the right to appeal as well. . . [T]his requirement means that a student found innocent in a hearing may be retried, even if the charges against him or her have already been proven baseless.[32]

The new guidelines also present a threat to campus free speech, according to the FIRE report. The Dear Colleague letter failed to mention that universities are obligated to respect the free speech rights of students. It also failed to clarify the distinction between provable harassment and protected speech. According to the speech advocacy group, this lack of clarification allows colleges to pursue "vague and overly broad sexual harassment policies" that run the risk of squashing the free speech rights of students.[33]

Yet it appears schools didn't heed the warnings of FIRE in the ensuing years. Many sexual assault cases that occur on campus are decided within university administrative hearings, not in the justice system. With a lower standard of proof needed and panels featuring untrained students and school officials, this system, unsurprisingly, makes terrible rulings.

Multiple innocent young men have found themselves expelled from school due to these incompetent hearings. A few famous examples include Drew Sterrett, a University of Michigan undergrad who was expelled after being found guilty of rape by his school—even though there was an abundance of evidence showing he was engaged in consensual sex. The ruling was later nullified three years after his expulsion, in 2015.[34] Another prominent example is Caleb Warner, a student at the University of North Dakota. In 2010, Warner was expelled after being found guilty by the school under the nebulous "preponderance of evidence" standard. It took over a year for UND to reverse its decision. However, the local police department had already taken action in the case at the same time that Warner was expelled—against his accuser, for filing a false police report.[35]

Possibly the worst example of this procedure comes from the University of Tennessee–Chattanooga. Corey Mock was a student and wrestler for UTC when he met up with Molly Morris at a house party in spring 2014. The two hooked up after the party. Months after the encounter, Morris claimed to school officials that she was given a spiked drink and that Mock had raped her. It was a classic he said, she said case, with little proof an actual crime was committed, yet administrators dawdled over whether they should expel Mock. His first hearing, in June 2014, resulted in a decision to clear him of any wrongdoing. Then a letter of reconsideration was filed by the accuser, which apparently convinced the presiding administrator, Joanie Sompayrac, to overturn her initial ruling in August and expel Mock from UTC. He was later reinstated after appealing the decision. When the school learned that *Vice* was investigating the case in November, they removed him from the wrestling team and then eventually expelled him before the article ran in December.[36]

In 2015, a Tennessee judge overruled the school's final decision, stating in her decision that UTC's actions were "arbitrary and capricious." "The UTC Chancellor improperly shifted the burden of proof and imposed an untenable standard upon Mr. Mock to disprove the accusation that he forcible assaulted Ms. Morris," Judge Carol McCoy ruled at the time.[37]

If the handling of these cases were not bad enough, the state of California wants to make them worse through affirmative consent laws. Proposed to handle the apparent, previously alluded to problem of "No Means No" consent laws, affirmative consent aims to make "Yes Means Yes" the standard. Not only would a man have to receive very explicit permission to engage in sex, but he would have to continually ask for verbal consent to continue intercourse throughout its duration. If not properly done, he could be charged with rape. California made this principle state law in 2014.

After it became state law, *Vox* editor-in-chief Ezra Klein

penned an absurd defense of the standard. Accepting the one-in-five figure as a horrifying fact, Klein argued that the bill was needed in order to terrify men into submission.

> If the Yes Means Yes law is taken even remotely seriously it will settle like a cold winter on college campuses, throwing everyday sexual practice into doubt and creating a haze of fear and confusion over what counts as consent. This is the case against it, and also the case for it. Because for one in five women to report an attempted or completed sexual assault means that everyday sexual practices on college campuses need to be upended, and men need to feel a cold spike of fear when they begin a sexual encounter.[38]

Just what college campuses need—more confusion over what constitutes a rape. Naturally, the law poses a dire threat to due process and opens up the possibility of more innocent men being punished over false allegations. Even if a male follows affirmative consent to a tee, he can still find himself expelled under the terrible system of college-administrated justice. That happened to a University of Massachusetts–Amherst student who was banished from school after a girl he hooked up with claimed she could not remember giving consent. The decision was made in spite of the male stating he had continually asked for permission throughout the disputed interaction.[39]

The obsession with rape culture is not due to a desire to resolve a nationwide crisis. It's a propaganda tool for feminists to capture power. For third-wave feminists, the goal is to make women the dominant gender on a college campus, giving them an environment where they can "have fun" with little consequence. Prominent feminist and *Guardian* columnist Jessica

Valenti made the case for such a scenario in a 2014 column titled "Real Equality Is When Women Have the Right to Be as Drunk and Stupid as Men."

> Do we really believe that women shouldn't have the freedom to get drunk and be stupid? That they can't partake in the silly, fun, dumb behavior that we've come to expect of young people—young men—on the brink of adulthood? That one bad decision and they could "get themselves" raped, but that never making a bad one will protect them?[40]

One of the proposed means for transferring power from men to women on a college campus is the advocacy for sororities hosting parties. All twenty-six sororities of the National Panhellenic Conference ban alcohol in their houses. However, some would like that to change so women can become the sexual "gatekeepers" on campus. "That would mean that there would be women at the door, and they would decide if you were gentlemanly enough and trustworthy enough to come into your party," "masculinity expert" Michael Kimmel told the *Atlantic* in 2015 of why sororities controlling parties is a great idea. "Think of all the social pressure on [the men]."[41]

The idea gained renewed attention after the release of the raunchy 2016 comedy *Neighbors 2: Sorority Rising*. The plot of the Seth Rogen vehicle revolves around a rogue sorority hosting wild parties and consuming tons of alcohol and drugs. For this brave comedic innovation, the film was dubbed a feminist classic and prompted questions as to why sororities shouldn't be the primary hosts of college parties. "When we started researching how sororities work, we were shocked at how sexist the system was," *Neighbors 2* cowriter and producer Evan Goldberg said during a promotional interview. So the film decided to upend that apparent sexism. "There's some beauty in the fact that within the confines of an R-rated studio comedy sequel, the battle for gender equality in America is embodied by a group of college students flinging their bloody tampons at Seth Rogen," the *Daily Beast* glowingly reported. "Young women want and deserve places of their own to explore, feel safe, form bonds, and yes—also drink, do drugs, and have sex, on their own terms."[42]

Who would've thought the great moral crusade of our time would have been for young women to do as many drugs and have as much promiscuous sex as they want "on their own terms"?

The problem is those terms are incredibly convoluted, and having the power to control parties and punish men for not asking for consent every minute will not likely solve the underlying problems of campus sex confusion. Young women are encouraged to drink profusely and explore their sexuality to their hearts' content, yet these are the factors most responsible for the miserable experiences that propel campus rape hysteria.

On the drinking culture cause, some feminists, such as the *Bustle* writer previously mentioned, understand it as a major contributor to higher education's sex problem. But feminists do not like it at all for anyone to make the logical conclusion that girls should be more careful around alcohol and drink less to avoid uncomfortable experiences. Liberal writer Emily Yoffe argued for this idea in multiple articles at *Slate*, and received a tidal wave of backlash in response.[43]

"This is the very definition of rape culture. And it is so completely tired," *Salon*'s Kate McDonough wrote in 2013 of

Yoffe's suggestion. That critique hysterically argued that Yoffe had engaged in victim blaming and refused to point the finger in the proper direction: men. Instead of teaching women to act responsibly in volatile situations, the real solution is to teach men not to rape.[44]

In a perfect world, where people immediately learn and live out lessons like that, it would be the only solution to the problem. But in a society where we do not count on robbers not robbing and murderers not murdering, we must expect to take steps to ensure crimes do not happen to us instead of putting all the onus on the criminals themselves. Like locking your doors at night, watching how much you drink is sensible—particularly if you want to avoid regrettable and/or nonconsensual sex.

Drinking is a choice. Yet, the studies including many cases of drunken sex imply that women should not be held responsible for what happens while they are intoxicated. If we accept that way of thinking, then women should not be charged with driving under the influence if they claim they can't remember putting the keys in the ignition. Teach cars not to turn on, not women to stop drinking!

Of course, if a woman is violated while unconscious or after being drugged against her will, that's a crime. But to expect women to not give some regard to their own safety invalidates the American value of personal responsibility. We don't live in a perfect world, and we can't expect bad people to comport themselves to letting women live out their feminist duty to get plastered with no consequence.

The sexual promiscuity encouraged by feminists also comes with negative consequences. In the famous "Boys on the Side" essay, Hanna Rosin declared that "feminist progress right now largely depends on the existence of a hookup culture." The progress comes in the form of women having the ability to have as much sex as they want without the hazard of "overly serious suitors[s]." Committed relationships are a fatal problem because they could jeopardize "promising" futures, according to Rosin.[45]

But while it may lead to "progress," the studies reveal that the hookup culture is leaving women brokenhearted. The American Psychological Association's study on sexual hookup culture found that it led to a great abundance of guilt and negative feelings among its participants. Women in particular were far more likely to express negative feelings after a hookup.[46] Other studies show that instead of casual, no-strings-attached sex, women prefer serious, monogamous relationships.[47] Firsthand accounts of college hookup culture reinforce this overlooked sentiment. In a widely shared essay, recent college grad Leah Fessler explained how she and her friends felt hurt by the casual sex and no-commitment relationships they engaged in. She wrote that she would much rather have a traditional relationship, and her own study of her campus found her female peers shared the same desire. "My friends and I didn't just want to hook up. In fact, we *hated* hooking up. We wanted commitment, labels, love. We wanted real, live, official relationships," the young woman recalled.[48]

That leads us to what may be at the root of the concern over campus rape culture: there are fewer men for these young women to have monogamous relationships with. The factor that arguably plays the largest role in the feeling of oppression among college women, but is never mentioned, is the declining number of men attending universities. In 2013, the gender ratio within American higher education's graduating class was 57 percent female, 43 percent male. The Department of Education estimates that by 2023 the gap will grow to three women for every two men.[49] That disparity favors the men on campus in giving them a higher value due to their scarcity. Women have less power to demand the romance and commitment Fessler desires when the men have multiple options for sex. Fraternity men are especially gifted in this regard owing to their higher status and the many social functions that give them access to dozens of coeds.

It's no surprise then that some of the most famous college rape allegations stem from girls rejected by their suitors. Jackie Coakley concocted her twisted gang-rape fantasy initially as part of an elaborate plot to win over a male friend who refused to date her. Emma Sulkowicz made a rape allegation against Paul Nungesser after he stopped returning her texts following a consensual sexual encounter.

Imagine how many allegations there will be when the gender gap widens even further.

The education gender gap is a problem far larger than American higher education and is rooted in issues within our nation's primary education system. Fixing that specific problem is beyond the scope of this work. However, campus feminists are not doing their female peers any favors by creating an atmosphere hostile to men. Millennial women seem to want the same things out of relationships that their mothers and grandmothers wanted. With fewer male partners available, pushing forward outrageous affirmative consent laws and other intrusive measures appears to be a case of cutting off your nose to spite your face.

The tragedy of contemporary feminism is that the things it

is outraged by are a result of women's incredible progress in this country. Females dominate college campuses and will soon be overrepresented in an array of powerful professions. But with progress comes more demands. Proposals to "solve" campus rape culture is all about amassing power, not making universities safer. The freedom to punish men for any offense a woman finds to be sexual assault is a power like no other. Feminists want college men to feel that chill Ezra Klein spoke about so they will accept a submissive role in gender relations.

The frivolous nature of third-wave feminism isn't so frivolous when you see their goal as not equality, but supremacy over men. No more mansplaining, manspreading, or slow texting. Shut up and give up your seat if a woman asks you to, because her voice is more important.

The inequality desired by feminists is of course not going to lead to happier lives for the average women they are supposedly fighting for. All it means is that men are going to have to live with an unfair standard that benefits no one except the most die-hard activist.

Sadly, rape culture hysteria is likely to remain as strongly entrenched as ever, with fewer men on campus and jilted women feeling justified in filing rape charges against the poor fellows who fail to answer their texts in a timely manner.

7

GREEKS UNDER SIEGE

A university can be an intimidating place for freshmen. Whisked away from the friends and communities they've known all their lives, new arrivals face a lonely world full of strangers and unfamiliar surroundings.

For years, colleges have offered dozens of groups and associations for students to join to overcome the isolation that can happen at a large campus. And no student community is more popular in making a campus feel like home for thousands of young adults than Greek life. At the same time, no student community is more hated by the campus Left.

Before proceeding, let me clarify that the only Greek organizations the campus Left are upset with are the historically white ones—nearly all of whom are either associated with the North-American Interfraternity Conference (for fraternities) or the National Panhellenic Conference (for sororities). Social justice warriors seem at peace with the historically black fraternities and sororities of the National Pan-Hellenic Council (better known as the "Divine Nine") and the various "multicultural" Greek organizations that cater to various nonwhite ethnic groups.

Previous chapters have mentioned the allure of vicious identity politics for the college kid trying to find a meaning to his life, connecting one with others on a deeper level than mere study pals. In the same vein, fraternities and sororities offer a nonpolitical, more inebriated alternative to the dreary world of identitarian agitation.

Ever since the nineteenth century, fraternities and sororities have been a common feature at American college campuses. Few universities are without the Greek-lettered houses that dot the areas surrounding any given campus. These groups offer numerous activities for young people—from intramural sports to philanthropic endeavors to social events. Of course, the part fraternities and sororities are most famous for is the social aspect.

Greek organizations, particularly fraternities, have the reputation for amounting to nothing more than debauched drinking clubs. People only join these groups to party, and there's nothing to gain from them outside of a good time. Fraternity members just spend their entire days guzzling liquor and causing massive headaches for their deans; so goes the stereotype. We can thank popular films such as *Animal House* for this reputation.

While this stereotype has some basis in reality, the wild parties are not the sum of the Greek experience. The feeling of brotherhood/sisterhood is a primary driver for recruitment to these organizations. People want to belong somewhere, and it doesn't hurt when that sense of belonging comes with a keg or two.

So why are fraternities and sororities facing additional scrutiny for trying to offer kids a place to find community amid the overwhelming weight of college life? What's the harm in letting kids have a little bit of fun before they're set off into the real world?

There's great harm in letting these groups exist as they are, the campus Left would contend. Unlike the Black Lives Matter crowd, fraternities and sororities don't represent the multicultural vision of the New America. Instead, they represent the bad, old America—with all its patriarchy, toxic masculinity, repressed women, white privilege, and sinister lack of diversity. Not to mention they exclude those who are not members of the social circle, making Greek life an elitist bastion in a sea of artificial inclusivity.

Granted, some of the major threats to Greek life do not come from overzealous administrators or their left-wing peers. The insurance costs for keeping fraternities and sororities are going through the roof thanks to hazing and poor risk management at parties. Nothing can get a fraternity kicked off campus faster than a provable claim of hazing, and in the age of cell phones, it's becoming easier for the evidence to reach administrators' desks. The excesses of wild partying are also stacking up, with organizations that host parties more liable than ever to be sued for any injury or death that may occur as a result.[1]

While the hazards of partying and hazing pledges make Greek organizations ripe for dismissal, that doesn't explain why they've become a target of their fellow students. In fact, the campus Left has no problem with casual sex and binge drinking. Many feminists encourage those activities for young women as a way to smash the patriarchy. Hazing among traditionally black fraternities is considered far worse than that of their white counterparts,[2] yet they are pretty much entirely ignored by social justice warriors.

Fraternities and sororities offer a traditionalist alternative to the college stereotype at a time when campuses are descending into left-wing madhouses. For that reason, along with their unbearable whiteness, these organization are put into the cross-hairs of left-wing activists.

To many students, the ideas of their professors and fellow students are incredibly bizarre and they want no part of them. In the safe confines of the fraternity house, life can go on without gender-neutral pronouns, white-privilege checking, and lectures on "toxic masculinity." Young adults can vote Republican, uphold traditional gender roles, wear preppy clothes, and fly the American flag to their hearts' content—and maintain these traits as the social norm. Students may initially be drawn in by the party, but they stay for the culture of Greek life.

A penchant for conservative politics can be discerned from the tone of popular frat websites such as Total Frat Move and Old Row, which show ample support for right-wing ideas and contempt for political correctness. Way back in the 1960s, Sen. Barry Goldwater reportedly noticed the conservative nature of Greek life and remarked, according to legend, "Where fraternities are not allowed, communism flourishes."[3]

The symbolism of fraternities and sororities draws heavily upon the history and religion of Western civilization. Fraternities sport coats of arms reminiscent of medieval knightly orders, brandish titles drawn from the Roman Republic, and maintain Greek and Latin mottos, clear throwbacks to the days when classical learning dominated American education.[4] The Bible provides a major influence for sorority and fraternity rituals. Many fraternities—such as Sigma Alpha Epsilon, Kappa Alpha Order, and Pi Kappa Alpha—express pride in their founding roots in the South, and Greek life has a particularly strong presence at Southern schools.

Kappa Alpha Order takes their Southern pride the farthest in having Gen. Robert E. Lee as an honorary founder and hosting Old South Balls. The balls require the men to dress like traditional Southern gentlemen, sometimes decked out in Confederate officer garb, and the ladies to dress up like Southern belles. Old South Balls are, naturally, despised by the campus Left, and they routinely draw protests. In response to the constant criticism over the social functions, KA's national organization banned the wearing of Confederate outfits.[5]

Besides providing a safe space for traditional Western civilization in an ocean of postmodern puritanism, fraternity and sorority members are likelier to graduate than their non-Greek peers and are, on average, more engaged in their adult jobs than those who did not go Greek.[6]

Groups such as fraternities and sororities embody the all-American principle of freedom of association. Young people organize themselves independently of the school and pick who they want to be in the groups on their own terms. The courts recognize this freedom as a fundamental element of the First

Amendment's guarantee of free speech protection.[7] You cannot effectively express an opinion if you are barred from joining with other like-minded folks in pushing that viewpoint. As social organizations, fraternities and sororities, by nature, will admit students they believe will fit into their culture rather than subscribing to quota dictates set by campus administrators.

Free association is essential to a country that prides itself on maintaining a vibrant civil society. With fraternities and sororities, young people are able to participate in something greater than themselves, engage with their community, and learn the basics of civic responsibility. Joining a frat is a much better option for a freshman than the alternative of hunkering down in his dorm and playing video games all day.

There are a few restrictions on how fraternities and sororities can limit their membership, however. For instance, they cannot discriminate based on race. In the past, many fraternities and sororities had "white clauses" spelled out in their membership requirements, but all of these groups had eliminated these discriminative standards by the 1960s.[8] Without those restrictions, the organizations affiliated with the North-American Interfraternity Conference and the National Panhellenic Conferences still have a "white" reputation though. That, naturally, is a serious outrage to the Left.

Though the exact data on racial makeup is scarce, the few figures available do show these groups as primarily composed of white members. At Princeton University, an Ivy League school with a liberal reputation, 73 percent of all fraternity members and 77 percent of sorority members were white, while less than 50 percent of the school's attendees were white.[9] A 2010 study conducted of eight historically white Greek organizations at three different East Coast universities found that they were, on average, 96 percent white.[10]

Two major controversies recently threw the unbearable whiteness of Greek life into the public spotlight. The first occurred at the University of Alabama at the start of its fall 2013 semester. Two African-American freshmen participated in sorority recruitment week—known as rush—in the hopes that one of the sixteen organizations they met with would give them a bid to pledge. None of the sororities—which all lacked black members at the time—offered the chance for membership to the black hopefuls. Scandal soon erupted when it was discovered that one of the two girls was allegedly turned down by a sorority because of her race. According to the Alabama school newspaper, the *Crimson White*, members of Alpha Gamma Delta said the active undergraduate sisters wanted to give a bid to the stellar black rushee, but alumnae had thwarted their efforts. The reason for the reluctance: the alumnae advisory board wanted to keep the sorority exclusively white.[11]

Outrage quickly followed the publication of the report, and hundreds of students outside of Greek life marched on campus to demand the integration of fraternities and sororities. The controversy grabbed the attention of the state's governor, Robert Bentley, who insisted that Greek organizations must do more to increase the diversity of their membership. Professional race hustler Jesse Jackson even flew down to Tuscaloosa to join in the festivities and to tell demonstrators, "What's at stake here is your future, not the traditions of *their* past." Jackson urged students to picket all sorority houses until they agreed to have a sufficient level of diversity.[12]

A week after the scandal first erupted, Alabama's sororities offered bids to fourteen non-whites, eleven of whom were African-American. Six of the minority girls who were offered membership accepted the bids. The move was greeted as an event almost as monumental as the original integration of the university back in 1963. *Time* magazine wrote of the development with the headline "University of Alabama Moves to End Segregated Sorority System" and the subhead "After more than a century of discrimination—and a week of bad publicity—the school will allow black women to join white sororities."[13]

The article from America's flagship newsweekly shows the embarrassingly inaccurate coverage of the incident. For one, a black student had already been accepted into a historically white Alabama sorority ten years before the national scandal. Second, the organizations had no restrictions based on race outside of the word of a few backward alumnae—and the school especially did not mandate any form of segregation when it came to these chapters. Third, almost all of the coverage overlooked how Alabama's historically black Greek organizations had not admitted a white student into membership for several years—a fact, along with the mention of the first black student to join an Alabama sorority, reported by the very article that launched the controversy.

But those inconvenient truths were virtually ignored in favor of bemoaning the perpetuation of white supremacy within Alabama's Greek life fifty years after the segregationist governor George Wallace made his stand in front of the schoolhouse door. *Vice*'s documentary on the story was titled "Racist Sororities at Alabama" and made a point of negatively comparing the school's evil Greek life with that of its noble-hearted multicultural intellectual living program. The film hammered in the idea that these Greek organizations were too white and actively discriminated against minorities, with little concrete evidence outside of the recruitment story.[14] That message, delivered by the national media, prompted UA's student government to pass a meaningless resolution urging its historically white fraternities and sororities to integrate—something they had already done many years earlier.[15]

The *Vice* documentary shows the contempt for these groups was not going to go away with the "integration" announcement. The student members of the Mallet Assembly, the intellectual living center positively portrayed in the report, remained dissatisfied with the apparent progress, implying that what they really wanted was a radical transformation of the fraternities and sororities. No more preppy clothes. No more Republican politics. And certainly no more expressions of Southern pride. Just celebrations of equality and diversity, like the Mallet Assembly puts on.

The lingering ill will toward Alabama fraternities and sororities manifested itself two years into the uproar over one group's recruitment video. The Alpha Phi sorority chapter at Alabama released a five-minute video of their sisters doing stereotypical sorority-girl things. Mainly they frolicked around in nice outfits and had a blast for all five minutes of the clip. The clip is so inoffensive (outside of the obnoxious music) that it boggles the mind that anyone would find it an outrage. But since we live in a crazy age, people did become enraged at the sight of young women having harmless fun. An Alabama writer named A. L. Bailey shrieked over the horror of the Alpha Phi video in a column that went viral in August 2015. "It's a parade of white girls and blonde hair dye, coordinated clothing, bikinis and daisy dukes, glitter and kisses, bouncing bodies, euphoric hand-holding and hugging, gratuitous booty shots, and matching aviator sunglasses," Bailey lamented. "It's all so racially and aesthetically homogeneous and forced, so hyper-feminine, so reductive and objectifying, so Stepford Wives: College Edition. It's all so . . . unempowering." In his opinion, girls enjoying themselves without an adequate amount of diversity and feminist-approved clothing is "worse for women than Donald Trump."[16] So, instead of looking good while somersaulting, these young women should get super serious and build a "united front for empowerment." What the heck that means is not explained, but it's easy to understand Bailey's message: these sorority girls shouldn't be so white and feminine.

That one opinion caused such a negative reaction that UA's administration formally condemned the Alpha Phi video. "This video is not reflective of UA's expectations for student organizations to be responsible digital citizens," a university spokeswoman said in a press statement on the video controversy.[17]

According to their superiors, sorority women need to ditch the traditional gender roles and stop being so homogeneous. Freedom of association be damned—it's time for all to meld into PC culture.

The abhorrent homogeneity of Greek life was highlighted a second time recently after a University of Oklahoma fraternity was caught on tape singing a racist chant. In early March 2015, a camera phone captured the seconds a dozen or so Sigma Alpha Epsilon brothers chanted on a party bus that there would never be a black member of their fraternity—in very racist language. The chant prominently featured the n-word and included a reference to lynching. The short clip soon came to the attention of the national press and spent a whole week as the outrage story. OU expelled the leaders of the chant and suspended the entire SAE chapter while campus protesters marched for more change.[18]

While the chant was indefensible and rightly deserved contempt from polite society, it was protected by the First Amendment and hardly amounted to a credible threat of violence. It was sung within the private confines of a party bus, and had it not been leaked, it would have never been known of. Ugly language, yes. A serious threat, no. UCLA law professor and *Washington Post* blogger Eugene Volokh argued for this very same point and warned OU's administrators that it was likely against the law to punish fraternity brothers for their (poorly thought-out) free expression.[19] The university expelled the two SAE brothers for their "leadership role in leading a racist and exclusionary chant which has created a hostile educational environment for others." Volokh found this justification a disturbing precedent for censorship of other, constitutionally protected viewpoints on campus.

> There is, as I've mentioned before, no First Amendment exception for supposed "hate speech." But if there is such an exception, there certainly is no First Amendment foundation for distinguishing speech that is actually or supposedly anti-black from speech that is anti-white, anti-Semitic, anti-Muslim, anti-Catholic, anti-women, or anti-men. If the University of Oklahoma president's position is accepted as legally sound, then there'd be no legal basis for protecting the other kinds of speech while expelling students for this sort of speech.[20]

The rest of the media, however, did not share Volokh's

concern and cheered on OU's harsh reaction to the chant. Additionally, the press spent the rest of March blowing up any instance of an American fraternity doing anything racially insensitive.[21] A few commentators urged the federal government to do a thorough investigation of Greek life and revoke the tax-exempt status of the groups the feds determine are racist.[22] The focus of the investigations would be on the historically white organizations—not the groups designed primarily for blacks and other minorities. Because we all know their lack of diversity and racial pride is not a problem, for some reason.

Race is not the only issue fraternities and sororities are criticized for on college campuses. The primary villain in rape culture hysteria are fraternities, as amply demonstrated by the 2014 University of Virginia gang rape hoax. When one fraternity stood accused of gang raping a freshman girl as a pledge ritual, as claimed by a *Rolling Stone* magazine article, the school immediately suspended all frats for the remainder of the fall semester. An endless stream of news articles was released that declared fraternity houses were rape centers.[23] One intrepid UVA law student even argued that the gang rape accusation made it abundantly clear that fraternities operated as organized crime outfits. Thus, they should be prosecuted under laws created to bring down the Mafia.[24]

Eventually, the tale of gang rape was proven to be nothing more than the twisted fantasy of a disturbed mind and the national furor subsided. But before UVA would allow its fraternities to come back from their suspensions administered over false pretenses, the school made them agree to stringent standards concerning parties. The new regulations would require fraternities to have "sober brothers" to pour all drinks and guard access to the house's rooms. It also required frats to procure security and maintain guest lists for all social events at their houses. Two traditionally Southern UVA fraternities—Alpha Tau Omega and Kappa Alpha Order—refused to sign the agreement because it was based on a fabricated story. While the university admitted the rape hoax had been "discredited," their new standards showed they thought their Greek organizations still promoted a rape culture.[25]

So far, the few incidents of racial insensitivity and false rape claims have not amounted to an existential threat to Greek life. But the development that may radically alter fraternities and sororities is the severe infringement upon freedom of association known as "all-comers" policies. An all-comers policy stipulates that campus groups cannot make belief-based choices when it comes to granting membership and selecting leaders. Groups are mandated to welcome all interested parties into the group, no matter if those parties' beliefs are in opposition to the values of the organization.

The policy has mostly been adopted to force Christian groups—which often require adherence to biblical teachings to attain membership—to let in students who don't adhere to their beliefs. The Foundation for Individual Rights in Education has called the policy a threat to free association because it forces groups to forsake cherished values in order to comply with it.[26]

A 2010 Supreme Court decision upheld the legality of these policies in a case over a Christian student group at Hastings College trying to tie membership to faith. The court ruled the college could invalidate that clause and force the group to accept any applicant—regardless of that person's beliefs. The most infamous case of the all-comers policy occurred at Vanderbilt

University. Controversy arose in late 2010 after Beta Upsilon Chi, a Christian fraternity, kicked out gay members allegedly due to their sexual orientation.[27] The subsequent uproar on campus prompted Vanderbilt to dust up on a long-standing nondiscrimination policy and start strictly enforcing it the following academic year. The primary groups affected were political and religious groups who had to open up membership to people with opposing views. Many Christian groups decided to go off-campus to avoid the policy, and the school's starting quarterback at the time, Jordan Rogers, publicly criticized the policy for undermining the mission of his group, the Fellowship of Christian Athletes.[28]

The one notable part of the student community that was exempt from the policy was fraternities and sororities. While that exception may mean an all-comers policy would have no effect on Greek life if enforced, it actually does have a substantial, slippery-slope effect on the very foundation of fraternities and sororities: free association. Greek organizations are built on having the freedom to discriminate based on sex and other selection criteria. It's a clear double standard to exempt fraternities and sororities from the dictates of all-comers, as admitted by the *Fraternal Law Newsletter*, a periodical dedicated to legal issues surrounding Greek life, in its condemnation of Vanderbilt's policy.

> While the Greek world has long benefitted from federal law that recognizes that college social fraternities and sororities may discriminate in their membership policies on the basis of sex, that exemption applies only to federal anti-discrimination law. It does not prevent even a public university from imposing its own anti-discrimination policies to deny recognition to a Greek group that

discriminates on the basis of gender.[29]

Currently, fraternities and sororities have not been impacted by college antidiscrimination policies. But if demands for more diversity and inclusion continue, it's very possible imposed quotas will come down hard on Greek organizations. The exclusive and homogeneous reputation of Greek life will still insult campus SJWs, and their continued existence is enough of an incentive to radically mold them to conform to left-wing dogmas.

It should come as no surprise then that the rumblings of campus backlash are starting to emerge within the Greek community. The "#TheChalkening" phenomenon mentioned in the introduction was driven mainly by fraternity brothers who had had enough of political correctness. The popular online fraternity brand Old Row encouraged its supporters to draw pro-Trump messages at their college and has repeatedly highlighted the excesses of campus insanity.[30]

With straight, white, conservative men and women serving as the arch-villains of the campus Left's imagination, the fury directed against those who resemble the stereotype will only increase. Whether besieged fraternities and sororities will band together for something more important than a booze-soaked date party and stand up against those who wish to eradicate their prized traditions remains to be seen.

8

ART OF THE HOAX

One of the defining features of campus insanity is the sheer number of falsehoods and flat-out hoaxes that have been promoted on behalf of social justice.

The "1 in 5 women are sexually assaulted in college" figure is continually bantered around, even though it does not reflect reality. Black students claim they face racism on a daily basis because they imagined they saw a Klansman walking around on campus. False rape accusations are routinely believed and broadcasted before any investigation takes place.

Chapter 6 recalled some of the most notorious examples of social justice warriors falling for outright hoaxes. The most famous case of recent years was the University of Virginia gang rape hoax published by *Rolling Stone*. Nearly the entire country bought into the story, and UVA became embroiled in protests because it was thought that a fraternity got away with a brutal rape of an innocent girl. As previously shown, it was all a pack of lies told by spurned hoaxer Jackie Coakley, who created a fake suitor to fool her very *dis*interested love interest. The name of the fake character, Haven Monahan, was later given as the identity of her imaginary lead attacker.[1]

The tale was compared to the 2006 Duke lacrosse case, where three white members of the prestigious university's lacrosse team were charged with raping a black stripper. Like the UVA hoax, the rape claim turned out to be a lie of a mentally deranged woman (who later ended up going to jail for murdering her boyfriend) and was championed by a reckless prosecutor who exploited it for political gain.[2] But unlike the UVA case, the Duke hoax was ginned up to stoke racial tension in Duke's surrounding community rather than to legitimize the rape-culture delusions of feminists.

Rape-culture hysteria has encouraged many of its believers to buy into half-truths and distortions to buttress their cause. While few of the stories they have come to champion touch the hoax level of UVA's Jackie Coakley, they usually play fast and loose with the truth, as noted earlier.

What this chapter aims to highlight are the stories promoted by campus leftists that turned out to be certifiable hoaxes. The following list is not an exhaustive catalog of all reported hoaxes, but only a wrap-up of some of the most egregious and/or famous examples. It is discouraging to think campus leftists and their enablers have hitched themselves to lies time and time again. Yet it should be expected when they are taught to believe racism and bigotry are thriving, and desperately hunt out examples of injustice in their own communities.

YALE UNIVERSITY "WHITES GIRLS ONLY" FRATERNITY PARTY

Around Halloween 2015, a prominent student leader claimed in a Facebook post that black friends of hers were turned away from a house party hosted by the Sigma Alpha Epsilon fraternity because they weren't white. The only new arrivals SAE was letting in were white girls, supposedly. Coupled with a campus debate over culture-appropriating Halloween costumes, the claim of a racist frat party helped spark a wave of protests on campus. A viral video of angry students berating a college professor over his white privilege and the disruption of an event hosted by conservatives in support of free speech were all part of the uproar over the white-girls-only party.

However, a thorough investigation of the party by Yale officials revealed no evidence of racism on the part of SAE. There were in fact guests of all colors at the Halloween party. The event had so many guests, though, that they had to start restricting admission for late arrivals, which resulted in heated arguments between rejected attendees and fraternity members. But when officials looked at the evidence, they found no witnesses who could verify any SAE member said "white girls only" except for the original accusers.[3] In other words, one of the universities that witnessed the depth of campus insanity saw its privileged halls shaken over jilted guests venting their fury over not being let into a hot-ticket party for nonracial reasons.

THE KU KLUX KLAN INVADES MIZZOU

The notorious protests that engulfed the University of Missouri in fall 2015 were based on incidents that may not have their origin in reality. No one besides the student body president himself could verify that men in a Confederate flag–decked truck yelled the n-word at him. The true purpose of the infamous "poop swastika" found in a dorm bathroom was never discerned, and one wonders whether a sincere Nazi would draw his cherished symbol in feces. Video evidence showed that protest leader Jonathan Butler was not hit by the university president's parade car.[4] But while these incidents seem isolated and a tad dubious, together they were enough to bring down the president of Mizzou.

While these claims merit some degree of skepticism, the one definite hoax associated with the turbulence at MU comes in the accusation that the Ku Klux Klan invaded campus. As soon as the media began to sour on the protests following threats against journalists, the same student body president, Payton Head, who'd claimed he was called the n-word, posted on Facebook that the Klan was spotted on campus. Head said he had the fact confirmed and that he was working with the National Guard and state troopers to protect his fellow students. Furthermore, he cautioned all students to stay away from windows.

Following his post, other students began seeing Klansmen at Mizzou and reported hearing white power slogans and seeing bricks being thrown through dorm windows. Apparently, these students must have all been on the same drug, as the local police reported the KKK claim was totally unfounded. Head later apologized for seeing apparitions from the 1920s at his university.[5] The fact that anyone believed an organization that has long been irrelevant and boasts only three thousand members could take over a campus is ridiculous in the first place.[6] For the campus Left, no lie uttered seems too ludicrous to believe, and it wasn't the only time hysterical reports of the Klan invading a college campus have been made.

THE KLAN INVADES OBERLIN

Throughout the month of February 2013, Oberlin College, world renowned for its progressive reputation, witnessed a rash of mysterious racist posters and vandalism on its campus. Eventually, the culprits were caught—but not before the entire school went stark raving mad over the sighting of a Klansman wandering around on campus in the early morning hours of March 4, 2013. The sighting took place near the Afrikan Heritage House, leading many students to believe white supremacists were running loose around Oberlin.

The school canceled class for one whole day and hosted mandatory workshops on racism and sexism in the aftermath of the disturbing sighting. Oberlin alumna and comedian Lena Dunham tweeted out her despair at her alma mater suffering at the hands of hate. But the racist vandalism actually turned out to be the work of progressive, Obama-supporting pranksters. Both of the men expelled from Oberlin for the acts say they did it as a joke, and an investigation of their social media profiles by the *Daily Caller*'s Chuck Ross revealed them to be stereotypical Oberliners in their politics and religious views.

As for the roaming Klansman, police concluded it was most likely a woman walking around wearing a blanket.[7]

THE BUS BRAWL THAT FOOLED HILLARY

On January 30, 2016, three black female students at the University of Albany claimed they were viciously beaten on a bus by white passengers hurling racial slurs. "I just got jumped on a bus while people hit us and called us the 'n' word,'" Asha Burwell, one of the alleged beating victims, claimed in a tweet. "NO ONE helped us." The allegations set off outrage on campus and on social media, with protesters marching on campus for immediate action on the case. The incident reached the ear of Democratic presidential candidate Hillary Clinton, who tweeted out a link to the story on the bus beating, with the message, "There's no excuse for racism and violence on a college campus."

When police finally took a look at the bus's dozen video cameras, the story that emerged was quite different from what the three college students alleged had happened. It turns out the three "victims" were actually the ones who acted as the aggressors and assaulted their fellow bus passengers. Police found no evidence of racism in the incident, and charged all three for assault and making a false police report. The girls were expelled from Albany, and one later admitted to making up the hate crime.[8]

Clinton, for her part, never acknowledged or apologized for endorsing a hate crime hoax.

THE LOST BAR FIGHT HOAX

A University of Iowa student's night at a bar on April 30, 2016, turned into a nightmare when he was attacked without provocation and berated with racial epithets. This brutal hate crime left the black student, Marcus Owens, bruised for days, and activists saw the assault as an example of the brewing racial hatred within the campus town of Iowa City.

As in the Albany case, once police watched the security footage of the altercation, a different picture emerged of the night's events. Security footage showed that Owens was kicked out of the bar after becoming involved, of his own volition, in a massive brawl inside the establishment. Outside of the bar, he engaged in more physical altercations that he appeared to instigate but seemed to lose. One of the men he fought may have yelled the n-word in the heat of the moment. Law enforcement ruled that there was no racial bias involved in the melees Owens engaged in.

The hoaxer later apologized for his lies and blamed his actions on alcohol and the embarrassment of losing a fight.[9]

THE WHITE POWER NOOSE DRAWN BY BLACK STUDENTS

During Salisbury University's "Stop Hatin" week to promote diversity, a cruel drawing appeared on a whiteboard. The drawing depicted a hanging stick man with the word *nigger!* pointing at him, along with the hashtag #WhitePower. This racist drawing brought down a denunciation from school officials and hate crime investigation from the local police—who discovered it was drawn by two black students. Once the race of the students was identified, the investigation was dropped and the school announced they would not be expelled.[10]

THE ANTIBLACK SHOOTING THREAT OF SAGINAW VALLEY STATE

Following the hoopla at the University of Missouri and its own brand of hysteria, an anonymous post popped up on the social media platform Yik Yak on November 13, 2015, in which the user threatened to shoot "every black person I can on campus.

Starting tomorrow morning." The message was directed at the Michigan-based Saginaw Valley State University. The post caused concern in the community and police investigated.

The man behind the violent threat turned out to be an African-American named Emmanuel D. Bowen, who attended a nearby college. Shortly after posting the threat, he claimed it was done only to see how people would react to it. The law reacted to it by charging him with making a false report on a threat of terrorism.[11]

THE ANTIBLACK TWITTER ACCOUNT CREATED BY A BLACK ACTIVIST

In the middle of a November 2015 rally at Kean University in New Jersey, attendees were presented with some horrifying developments. A Twitter account with the handle @keanuagainstblk (standing for Kean University against Blacks) was making violent threats against all black students. "@kupolice I will kill all the blacks tonight, tomorrow and any other day if they go to Kean University," read one of the account's disturbing messages. Panic swept the campus as students were advised by the student body president to stay home and not travel on campus. Black ministers even petitioned to have the school's president removed over the death threats.

Funny enough, the person who made the threats was the same person who told everyone at the rally about it. Activist and Kean alumna Kayla-Simone McKelvey left the demonstration to go to a school library to create the hateful account. She then walked right back to the rally to deliver the shocking news. The purpose of the account was to generate more interest in racial issues, according to its creator. McKelvey publicly apologized for her hoax and served ninety days in jail over the death threats.[12]

THE WHITE-ONLY ART PROJECT

The State University of New York–Buffalo was riveted by the appearance of White Only and Black Only signs at campus bathrooms and water fountains in mid-September 2015. Students were immediately triggered by the signs, and many claimed they were traumatized by the sight. One student even declared the objects were an act of racist terrorism. The perp behind the signs was eventually revealed to be a black student who claimed he'd hung up the signs as part of an art project. He apologized for the "extreme trauma" his project caused, but did not apologize for doing it.[13]

THE SELF-MADE RAPE THREAT

The University of Wyoming was rocked near the end of its spring 2013 semester by an anonymous rape threat made on a UW Facebook page against a well-known progressive student, Meghan Lanker-Simons. "I want to hatef**k Meg Lanker Simons so hard. That chick runs her liberal mouth all the time and doesn't care who knows it. I think its so hot and makes me angry. One night with me and shes gonna be a good Republican bitch," the message read in all its ungrammatical glory. A rally was held in support of Lanker-Simons and to condemn the school's awful "rape culture." The school issued an official statement denouncing the anonymous rape threat and vowed to make sure the target felt safe on campus.

A police investigation of the threat found it to have been made by none other than Lanker-Simons herself. She was charged with interfering with a peace officer, but her legal troubles didn't deter her from pursuing her dream of attending law school after the hoax unraveled.[14]

THE GAY-BASHING FRATERNITY

A gay man walked into a fraternity party at the University of North Dakota one August night in 2015 and was kicked out. According to the "victim," Haakon Gisvold, he was thrown out of the party due to his sexual orientation, beaten, stripped, choked, and robbed by members of the Lambda Chi Alpha fraternity at UND. Once Gisvold made his allegation, the school suspended the fraternity. The Associated Press and other outlets picked up the story and sympathetically relayed Gisvold's allegations without any scruples. The assaulted man hoped that the fraternity members would learn from the experience and not just go to jail for it.[15]

As it turns out, Gisvold had a better chance of going to jail for falsifying information to police than the fraternity he accused of beating him. Police later determined the fight that occurred had nothing to do with anti-gay bias but with the alleged victim causing problems at the party and being asked to leave. Police wanted charges pressed against Gisvold, but the prosecutor declined to take it that far.[16]

THE GAY PROFESSOR WHO ASSAULTED HERSELF

A lesbian professor at Central Michigan University, Mari Poindexter, attended a Toby Keith concert on August 19, 2015, only to face extreme harassment from a man who accused her of being a "crossdressing fag." The man at first only swore at Poindexter with gay slurs, then ran into her at a bar after the show and punched her and spat in her face. Poindexter posted a photo of herself with a black eye on Facebook to announce to the world that she had suffered an assault. School officials publicly expressed solidarity with the victimized professor after her story became publicized.

As in nearly all of these cases, police eventually uncovered the truth after looking into the allegation. They checked video footage from the bar and found no evidence of the professor being the victim of an attack, or any other facts to support the allegation. As it happens, Poindexter gave herself the black eye to "raise awareness about the social hardships of people in the LGBTQ+ community." She was later sentenced to pay a fine of $225 and serve six months of probation for her hoax.[17]

THE GREAT NOOSE SCARE AT DELAWARE

University of Delaware students gathered for a Black Lives Matter campus protest on September 22, 2015, were horrified to find nooses hanging from trees near the event. Much shock and indignation followed. But police were able to reassuringly determine that the nooses were in fact the remains of paper lanterns from an event held months earlier.

Delaware activists did not buy the explanation, however, and insisted the school take immediate action against the hateful act of leaving paper lanterns in trees. Students claimed they still felt unsafe because of the non-hateful decorations, and a few administrators said the hoax, somehow, revealed the bigoted climate on campus.[18]

Never doubt the power of wanting to believe that a clear hoax still supports the idea that your campus is a cauldron of racism.

9

WHITHER WILL CAMPUS INSANITY TAKE AMERICA?

As we look upon the dilapidated state of higher education and its deplorable effects on the young, it's worth asking who's ultimately responsible for this madness.

Should we blame the professors who instruct students on the world and its history? Should we blame the parents who unleashed irrational and thin-skinned young adults onto society? Should we blame the unnecessary and intrusive college administrators who seem to serve no other purpose than catering to every whim of the campus radicals? Or should we blame the demonstrating students themselves, as they consciously chose to believe their ludicrous ideas and push for them in the real world?

The answer for who's most responsible for campus insanity isn't as simple as any of those suggestions. Among conservatives, the professors and deans receive the blame for why young kids embrace the radical fringes of the Left. This view envisions tens of thousands of eighteen-year-olds embarking on their journey into college with patriotic fervor and healthy, conservative values. Four years later, flag-waving Johnny is now flag-burning Johnny—all thanks to his sociology professor. "Even now, too few conservative parents realize how radical—and effective—the university agenda is," conservative commentator Dennis Prager said in a column that encapsulated the "evil professor" view. "They are proud that their child has been accepted to whatever college he or she attends, not realizing that, values-wise, they are actually playing Russian roulette, except that only one chamber in the gun is *not* loaded with a bullet."[1]

It is undeniable that many young people change their politics and values during their time in college. One of the reasons for that change is what they learn in class, which of course is determined by professors who overwhelmingly lean left. But the main problem with colleges isn't that they are churning out future Democratic voters who look down on their parents' conservative values. What is so disturbing about higher education is that it reflects the extreme fringe of trends already present in the rest of society.

Polarization is at an all-time high. Race relations are at an all-time low. Demonstrators march in the streets, demanding higher status before the law. Entitled celebrities are free to cry foul when online comments upset them and are instantly rewarded with victim status.[2] Corporate human relations work echoes that of microaggression patrols,[3] while the Fortune 500 kowtows to every request of the cultural Left.

Even professional football is not shielded from the growing tension in our society, as its 2016 Super Bowl halftime show featured a tribute to black power from pop singer Beyoncé.[4] The following NFL season witnessed several African-American players sit, kneel, or deliver a black power salute in protest against the national anthem.[5]

What's happening at campuses is not an isolated affair—it is a result of what is happening in America as a whole. The sense of shared values and culture among Americans is vanishing rapidly; at the same time many feel isolated from their communities and families.[6] Mass immigration has dramatically altered our country's demographics, while multiculturalism has created a confusing landscape of competing visions for what it means to be an American. Many citizens see our national society as one of millions of alienated atoms living in a continental strip mall, not interconnected denizens living happily together in one proud country.

Thus, they turn to alternative forms of identity. A real American identity—one not entirely composed of platitudes about "equality and opportunity"—is becoming a thing of the past. The ones who cling to it, as evidenced by Hillary Clinton's and the press's treatment of Donald Trump's supporters, are considered racist buffoons who need to die off.[7] The momentum of the present is veering toward tribalism, not unity. And the only thing keeping all the tribes of the Left unified right now is their shared animosity toward whites.

Higher education is just the place where this transformation is most apparent.

This virulent strain of identity politics is afflicting college campuses more so than any other part of society due to the unique circumstances of college campuses. Youth are renowned for their political energy and willingness to entertain extreme ideas. The cutting edge of the Left can always be discerned by what the kids are up to, and safe-space culture is the hot thing right now.

Another factor is that colleges are no longer simply places where students go to learn for four years. A subsidized commune for maturing adults is a more apt analogy for the role universities now serve, as students expect their schools to handle their personal issues and other matters in addition to providing them an education.

The expanded incentivization for engaging in identity politics at college campuses naturally encourages the radicalization of identity politics. Students gain admissions into college in many cases due to their race, so it follows that many of them would rely on that minority identity to gain more benefits in college. If they struggle in class because those racial preferences placed them into a school above their skill level, campus culture encourages them to blame racism instead of race-based admissions for their failures. Administrators are more than willing to buy into this theory of systemic racism and do everything in their power to eradicate the imaginary white supremacy of their campus to comfort the aggrieved.

Colleges are places where unmolded minds have the chance to hear from far-left professors and charismatic student-radicals for hours on end—increasing their risk for adopting loopy ideas. Along with that factor, you have thousands of strangers who haven't fully developed their capacity to handle emotions and difficult situations, all thrown together in one small community, giving rise to a multitude of possible conflicts.

That community and its student-driven culture are probably more responsible than the ramblings of professors for influencing students' views. Young folks want to fit in, and if the campus culture tells them they need to check their white privilege to be accepted, then they will do that. Peer pressure also keeps dissidents silent, as no one wants to earn the dreaded *racist* label.

How much further can this tumult go within higher education? As of September 2016, the college climate in general appeared to have more absurdity in store for America, and it could get even crazier at your nearest ivory tower.

Ultimately, the full elimination of campus insanity's poison would require massive cultural changes. Restoring an authentic national identity not dependent on empty platitudes would be a start. Undercutting the ideology of multiculturalism—which encourages Balkanization and separation from the national community—would also be a step in the right direction. Our society ceasing to feed into the Victimhood Olympics would send a strong signal to college kids to stop playing their own extreme version.

Those things would have to come from a change in cultural trends and cannot easily be altered by policy. The one legislative policy proposal that could stem the tide of minority identity politics on campus is one eliminating affirmative action.

As it is now practiced, affirmative action does nothing to make up for past injustices and only encourages its beneficiaries to dwell on those injustices. It incentivizes the embrace of destructive identity politics and race resentment. It does not foster intellectual, political, or socioeconomic diversity on campus. It prizes racial diversity above all else, while undermining America's commitment to a color-blind meritocracy. It even harms the people it tries to help by putting thousands of kids in schools in which they cannot succeed by only seeing their skin color in the admissions process.

A struggling student is more likely to vent his or her rage at the world through activism, thereby contributing to the vicious cycle of identity politics.

Forcing colleges to stop relying on racial preferences when it comes to college admissions would go far in stemming the tide of racial resentment in our country and on our campuses. No more rewards for playing minority identity politics. No more encouragement to feel that white supremacy is why a student is failing English lit. No more judging a student's worth based on his or her skin color. In order to move closer to that post-racial America that liberals dream of, you need to have a post-racial preferences admissions process.

There are certainly things that can be done in the short term without waiting for lawmakers to tear down affirmative action policy. Namely, college deans need to start punishing students who threaten the speech rights of their classmates, cease funding for left-wing programming, and stop catering to the demands of social justice warriors.

A few administrators have shown some backbone in dealing with campus protesters. One example is Ohio State University's threatening to arrest and expel any student who tried to occupy a university building in April 2016. The students in question responded to this threat by ending their protest.[8]

But while a handful of administrators are standing up

instead of bending the knee, it's clear that as a profession, they need some external motivation to start doing the right thing. Here are some proposals for achieving that goal.

STATE INTERVENTION

Nearly every college is dependent to some degree on government funding. Public colleges obviously stake their existence on receiving taxpayer funds. But so do private universities and for-profit schools, which heavily rely on federally funded student loans to keep the lights on. As evidence of this dependence, the for-profit behemoth ITT Technical Institute had to shutter its doors in 2016 after the Department of Education prohibited it from accepting students who were paying tuition with federal financial aid.[9]

Government, on both the state and federal levels, holds tremendous influence over universities with its power of the purse. Yet, so far, few lawmakers have proposed twisting the financial screws on universities to curtail the reckless behavior of campus protesters. Unfortunately, at the same time, more than a few legislators have fallen for the campus rape hysteria and devoted their time to investigating a hyperexaggerated phenomenon.[10]

There is one state assembly that has tried to strike back at the madness taking hold of their own universities, however. Tennessee's flagship state university and its premier private university have both been havens for prominent examples of campus insanity. When Vanderbilt University began enforcing its free association–killing all-comers policy, both state and federal lawmakers from Tennessee strongly condemned it for undermining the mission of Christian groups. The Tennessee General Assembly passed legislation in 2012 that would have forced Vanderbilt to remove its own policy, but it was vetoed by Republican governor Bill Haslam. Haslam claimed he had problems with the all-comers policy but felt the state bill violated his "limited government" sensibilities. "I think it is inappropriate for government to mandate the policies of a private institution," he stated in his veto message.[11]

Apparently that was a far worse prospect than a powerful institution grossly violating the American principle of free association. Nonetheless, some Tennessee lawmakers weren't deterred by that failure and there was an attempt the following year to strip Vanderbilt of its funding for on-campus police, though it didn't gain much traction.[12]

Tennessee legislators had far more success in dealing with the absurdities of its top public university. In the spring of 2013, the University of Tennessee–Knoxville was planning to host a "Sex Week"—which would feature a lesbian bondage expert and other enlightening speakers—in part with money from taxpayers. When Republican lawmakers in the Tennessee House heard of the event, the pressure they exerted was enough to convince the school to defund some of the programs associated with the week.[13]

Two years later, legislators once again had to step in and put university administrators in their place over ridiculous campus antics. When UT issued a "gender-neutral pronoun" guideline to students at the start of the fall 2015 semester, backlash forced the school to take it down from its website. Thirty-two state lawmakers sent a letter demanding to know why the university issued the guideline in the first place and planned committee hearings on how UT allocates its resources. Those hearings resulted in a brutal grilling of school officials as to why they feel the need to spend $5.5 million a year on diversity initiatives. The UT system president said it was spent in order to improve "the competency of our students."[14]

Lawmakers did not buy that explanation, and after UT's Office of Diversity and Inclusion sent out a directive advising students to root out any "secret" Christmas parties,[15] state representatives brought up legislation to cut off diversity funding for its public university system. The bill to defund diversity programs passed the assembly in 2016, and Governor Haslam signed this measure against campus insanity into law.[16]

The power of the purse is an effective tool to force college administrators to show some sense and spine when it comes to their disturbances. Defunding the looniest and most unnecessary of programs could stifle the dissemination of race resentment and identity obsessions. Some, such as libertarians, may object to the idea of the state interfering in the affairs of institutions such as universities—even when they are public. But that fails to consider how these large institutions wield incredible power over individual students and groups in a manner much more worrying than a state house cutting funds for sex weeks. A higher authority must put enough fear into administrators to stand up and not let young adults be indoctrinated with harmful ideas.

Of course, that's not the only way to strike fear into the hearts of college administrators.

THE POWER OF CHOICE

Boycotts are a time-honored tradition for showing your displeasure with an entity you disagree with. Hurting an institution at its pocketbook by personal choice rather than government intrusion comes off as a more American way of effecting change. With its potential to alter the behavior of its designated target, high school students and their parents protesting with their power of choice makes for a natural way to strike back at campus protesters and their administrative enablers. Why choose to go to a school that is notorious for suppressing speech and caving into Black Lives Matter agitators when there are other options available?

It appears many potential attendees of the University of Missouri asked themselves this question before deciding to go there for the 2016–17 academic year, much to the chagrin of MU. Mizzou suffered a nearly 25 percent drop in freshman enrollment that year after the campus witnessed a series of racial protests and administrative capitulation, leaving the school with a staggering $32 million windfall.[17] To offset the costs of campus radicalism, university officials announced a hiring freeze, the closing of several school dormitories,[18] and other cuts to keep the beleaguered college afloat.

On top of their admissions woes, donors cut back on their charitable giving to the university in response to the school's new reputation as an SJW headquarters.[19]

It is too early to tell whether this financial torture will change Mizzou's behavior and force it to correct its rep. But it made a noticeable mark on the school, and has added additional pressure to Mizzou to not have a repeat of what transpired the year before—all thanks to the power of choice.

Students are not locked into going to the big state school, especially if it's an awful place to be a white male walking around there. Where prospective students choose to go can depend on which universities choose to respect free speech and not let their crazies get out of hand. There are a few schools like Hillsdale College that intentionally seek to buck the trends of other universities and foster a classical spirit more in line with the olden days of higher education. But the key word about them is *few*, and not every student is going to attend one of these small schools.

The more realistic option is for parents and children to do their research into colleges' handling of minority identity politics and speech protection. The Foundation for Individual Rights in Education has an excellent rating system for how individual colleges treat free speech. It is a great resource for those who want to pick a college where they need not fear sharing their opinion. Green is for those who uphold the right, yellow is for those with some issues, and red is reserved for the outright speech suppressors.[20]

If these issues became a major part of the college selection process, more schools that encourage their students' destructive antics would face a similar fate as that of Mizzou, letting them know there are serious repercussions for bad behavior.

There is an even more radical idea than just selecting a college with a better reputation than the left-wing madhouse alternative: skip college altogether. That may sound ridiculous to those who still see a college degree as the ticket to the middle class, but the proposal has earned the persuasive support of one important backer: tech entrepreneur Peter Thiel. The Stanford graduate has long been a critic of higher education. In the 1990s he cowrote *The Diversity Myth*, which highlighted many of the issues plaguing college campuses today.[21] Thiel sees America's university system as comparable to the pre-Reformation Catholic Church in that it's a corrupt institution that hoards the keys to salvation. A metaphorical salvation, of course, but Thiel sees colleges' monopoly on degrees as just as bad as the Renaissance Vatican's control of indulgences.

To counteract this dominance, the billionaire is putting up his own money to pay brilliant teenagers to forgo college and start their own business instead. The first fellows of this program—each of whom received $100,000 to create a start-up—said the experience was incredibly rewarding, and the eighty-three fellows Thiel had backed by the year 2015 had launched projects that, in total, had earned $72 million in investments and $29 million in revenue.

While far too small and narrowly tailored to pose a serious challenge to university education, Thiel's effort is a sign that success can still be had without going down the mandated college path and its accompanying white privilege workshops.

STUDENT BACKLASH

For those unfortunate students who are stuck at an SJW-controlled college, there is still hope that they can make a difference without having to transfer. It just takes some initiative on their part to start confronting their campus activists and the capitulators who let them run wild. A protest movement in opposition to the prevailing left-wing campus current is very much possible and is essential to defeating it.

The Students for a Democratic Society did not go unchallenged by their fellow students in the 1960s as they had to contend with the conservative Young Americans for Freedom. The reaction for our era does not need to be as ideological or even conservative. It just needs to be willing to fight back against political correctness. There are already signs of a backlash emerging in the aforementioned #TheChalkening phenomenon and the sold-out college crowds for Milo Yiannopoulos. The momentum needs to keep churning in order to form a pressure group that administrators have to consider as least as much as the social justice warriors. If every time a dean canceled a speech or considered introducing a mandatory diversity course he had to worry about protests from right-leaning students, he would be more cautious in giving in to the madness.

There is already a large community on campus that has the capacity to serve as the counterpressure to left-wing agitators: Greek life.

Even though fraternities and sororities are the most hated student groups by campus demonstrators, and college deans seem to only grudgingly accept their continued existence, they still maintain an influential place within higher education. Schools depend on them for involvement in homecoming activities, student government, and a number of other things critical to a vibrant campus. Boycotting homecoming and using Greek life's leverage within student government to protest the ludicrous actions of their school would send a strong message against campus insanity. It would simply require a level of seriousness and a willingness for fraternities and sororities to work together. It would also require coordination with students outside of Greek life who have also had enough of PC culture to increase the effectiveness of their protests. If the demonization of fraternities and sororities continues unabated, these groups may have no other choice but to resist.

It is likely going to take a combination of all three ideas for colleges to change course and return to their purpose of educating young minds. We cannot simply hope that this latest version of campus insanity runs its course and higher education returns to normal on its own accord. There has to be an effort by those shocked by what they see happening to do something about it. Lawmakers, parents, and students can all do their part to push back at an insidious movement that threatens to tear asunder the fabric of this country.

If we don't do anything about it soon, we will all one day have to adjust to living in a god-awful safe space formerly known as the United States.

TRUMP WIN'S AND CAMPUS INSANITY

No one thought he could pull it off, but Donald J. Trump somehow managed to win the 2016 presidential election.

And, arguably, no one was more shocked by this result than American higher education. In spite of their status as young adults, college students returned to their preschool selves at the horrid news. The day after the election, Cornell University hosted a "cry in" for its students to come and express their intense sadness in a safe space. Chalk was provided to students to vent their negative feelings in a colorful fashion.

Dozens of other schools played host to similar affairs. Students hosted emotional marches—full of sobbing participants—in the early morning hours of November 9. Elite institutions, such as Columbia University and University of California–Berkeley, saw numerous members of their student bodies participate in distraught demonstrations, some of which blocked roads and prevented fellow students from getting to class. At other campuses students took their anger out on American flags, ripping and burning them to show contempt for the nation that voted differently from them.[1]

On top of thousands of students expressing their dismay at the election, professors and administrators offered to coddle them by canceling classes, rescheduling tests, and providing free counseling to the aggrieved.[2] A few schools have vowed to turn themselves into "sanctuary campuses" and resist any attempts by the federal government to enforce immigration laws.[3]

With that effect, you can now attend college without taking the SAT or burying yourself in thousands of dollars in debt. You can just prove to administrators you have no documentation to stay in the United States, and you will be given a home. In the 1960s, it was the students breaking the law to resist the government. Now the administrators are joining in on the action.

The reaction to Trump's victory was unprecedented. The level of hysteria and people's unwillingness to come to terms with reality is a new low. It's not like The Donald is the first president in recent history who is unpopular on college campuses. George W. Bush was reviled by young leftists during his presidency, and demonstrations against his administration were a common sight on campuses both big and small.[4]

But those outbursts fit into the standard American political mold of protesting the opposition party and its policies. It even took the form of marches and sit-ins without the predominance of teary-eyed histrionics. Bush may have been a fascist to protesters, but voting for him was not called a hate crime, and his mere presence was not seen as an incitement to racial violence. The language and style of opposing Bush was very much in the mold of traditional American progressivism—"Give Peace a Chance! Down with Capitalism!"

The language and style employed against Trump, on the other hand, is much more in line with the campus leftism detailed in the previous chapters. Trump is a threat to these students because they are oppressed victims—a sure sign of the prevalence of victimhood culture. A student citing how she feels unsafe because Trump, allegedly, threatens her due to her minority identity is a clear pitch to the moral code of the twenty-first-century university. These kids are victims of an oppressive system, and they deserve special rights to elevate them above their misery. Their whole identity as a protected minority—and the status it bequeaths—is dependent on the notion that they suffer more than the privileged (i.e. whites).

The arguments against Trump do not rely on reasonable assertions of political differences, but on identity concerns. "Trump makes me feel unsafe as a bisexual Latino" is all that's needed to make the case that the next president must be dethroned.

The fact that over 60 million people voted for the man and he won the election fair and square by the terms of our democracy are irrelevant points to the oppressed victims. Their concerns outweigh the right to free speech on campus. It makes sense that they would think their interests also trump the democratic process, especially when it was racist White America that voted for Trump.

It's no wonder Your Vote Was a Hate Crime has become a popular slogan among the protesters,[5] and it's only a matter of time until professors include "electing Trump" into the litany of sins committed against people of color by Caucasians.

To win an argument on a college campus, all one has to do is brandish your victim credentials to silence the opposition. The reaction to Trump is similar to how campus lefties protest against conservative speakers—just on a larger, nationwide scale. By playing the victim card, activists have been effective in shutting down speakers they disagree with.

Unfortunately for these agitators, the same tactics can't overturn the results of a democratic election.

So they're stuck wailing to submissive administrators who are at a loss as to how to mollify their students' woes, besides making their college a Trump-free sanctuary. Students who think their safe spaces can be extended outside of university grounds are in for a rude awakening when Trump moves into the White House—a development they are powerless to stop.

Regardless of whether you love or hate Trump, his presidential campaign amounted to a total repudiation of everything the campus Left stands for, which explains why they are so incensed over his victory. Time and time again, Trump was called upon to apologize for statements that offended pretty much every protected class in America. Some of his comments were, of course, vulgar, boorish, and/or remarkably insensitive, yet he never apologized for any of his words or actions (with the notable exception of his infamous remarks about grabbing a woman's genitalia[6]). Most of the comments which liberals and journalists demanded penance for, however, were over political topics, not locker room talk. Trump campaigned on such hot-button issues such as immigration, crime, and terrorism where discussion is often rigorously policed to avoid giving any offense. Trump ignored the guidelines of the sensitive and spoke out on these topics in a blunt style that appealed to millions of Middle Americans. His campaign was first launched on a strong condemnation of criminal illegal aliens. Liberal pundits and Democratic politicians lectured the future president that he must repent for the words he used about illegal immigrants. Trump refused their request, and kept up with his "no apology" stance on calling anchor babies "anchor babies," noting the existence of Islamic terrorism, and a host of other issues.[7]

He condemned political correctness as a virus killing the nation and resisted its dictates in his rhetoric.[8] Opposing political correctness was a core tenet of his campaign, which ended up appealing to millions of Americans who had had enough of speech suppression. The campus Left, which depends on the enforcement of political correctness to achieve their agenda, was none too pleased by this development.

Trump also rejected minority identity politics, failed to acknowledge his "white privilege," and ignored the phenomenon of "systemic racism"—in contrast to his opponent, Hillary Clinton.[9] Trump expressed pride in America's past—as captured by his Make America Great Again message—and felt no need to apologize for its history. Additionally, Trump happens to be a white male, which already makes him racist and privileged in the eyes of campus agitators.

Thus, that the antithesis of the campus Left is moving into the White House is an unprecedented horror for the movement.

At the time of writing this chapter, Trump is two months from becoming president, and he is already having a major effect on campus insanity. In the short-term, a Trump administration looks to radicalize college agitators even more. Likely scenarios arising in higher education include: demands that images and words of the president are banned from campus; students wearing pro-Trump gear are harassed and assaulted on a regular basis without serious consequence; stipulations are pushed to prohibit any right-leaning speaker from appearing on campus; American flags disappear entirely from campus grounds in order to not give offense; illegal immigrants are given full-ride scholarships just for being undocumented; and universities routinely cancel classes to protest various actions by the White House.

Campus lefties will double down on all their worst elements: identitarian warfare, speech suppression, diversity worship, anti-Americanism, white guilt tripping, and male shaming. In the short-term, campus insanity is likely going to get much worse under a Trump administration.

But that's where the silver lining comes in.

For one, you have a person who has spoken out against campus unrest in the White House[10]—with his party in control of the Senate, the House of Representatives, and a majority of state legislatures.[11] Disgust with events at college campuses could finally prompt a stern response from lawmakers. As mentioned in the final chapter, politicians threatening university budgets can force administrators to act against the illiberalism of campus demonstrators. Parents, with the encouragement of national figures, can boycott schools with notorious leftist reputations and can go to schools where support for the president is tolerated.

The very thought that lawmakers may have to make sure universities allow students to express support for this nation's president should be enough of a wake-up call to Americans that something is profoundly wrong in higher education. It should also strike right-leaning students as something they should stand up against as well. Trump became a symbol of resistance against tolerance earlier in 2016, and there's every reason he will remain one throughout his presidency. In this case, however, he can lend the moral weight of the presidency to the cause.

Trump supporters, or just even students fed up with political correctness, can begin to fight back against illiberal tolerance by taking up causes like flying the American flag and putting up pictures of the president on campus. These simple acts would gain wide support from the general population and any campus backlash would reveal the insanity of the other side. Students can gain easy victories if administrators unwisely try to suppress these activities and political pressure forces the deans to capitulate.

President Donald Trump presents the opportunity for radical changes in many aspects of America. Higher education is one such item, and while the news reports before he takes the reins of power look grim, the possibility of serious campus reform looks stronger than ever under a Trump administration.

Colleges are going to serve as one of the central battles in America's culture war for the next four years. If those who are sick of all the intolerance, hate and illiberalism of campus leftists, there may be no better opportunity in your lifetime to fight back than now.

Don't wait. Make American Colleges Great Again.

ACKNOWLEDGMENTS

To my family and friends who supported and helped me write this book, and provided the encouragement to continue on with the project.

A special acknowledgment to Tucker Carlson for encouraging me to write columns for *The Daily Caller*, which provided the impetus for this book. To those who have helped promote, edit, and make my work possible, I thank Vince Coglianese, Eric Owens, Paul Conner, Emma Colton, Peter Hasson, Blake Neff, and Alexander Pfeiffer.

Also, a note to gratitude to Annabel Scott and Kyle VonEnde for helping me with the notes and citations.

APPENDIX

THE GREAT COLLEGE SWINDLE

Campus unrest isn't the only problem facing higher education today. Every child is taught that he or she needs a college degree to succeed, but that degree is losing its value with every passing year. Massive student loan debt, worthless majors, and a total lack of preparation for the workforce are all hallmarks of a twenty-first-century college education. This chapter aims to note the other problems besetting colleges besides racial activists clamoring for victimhood status and embracing tribalism.

THE STUDENT LOAN CRISIS

The stereotypical pain of every twentysomething in America right now is the massive burden of student loan debt. At least 40 million Americans have outstanding student loan debt, amounting to a combined $1.2 trillion. Student loan debt affects the vast majority of recent college grads, as nearly 70 percent of those who receive a bachelor's degree walk out owing the federal government money. The average amount owed in student debt by the graduating class of 2015 was a whopping $35,051—the highest amount in history.[1] To put that in perspective, the average recent graduate is estimated to be only making around $36,000 a year. That means the average grad's student loan debt is basically equal to his or her yearly salary. The average hourly wage has actually fallen for graduates since 2000, and that's considering the $36,000 figure, which is probably skewed higher than the actual average.[2] Young adults are also found to have significantly lower earnings than the median income when compared with the twentysomethings of the recent past.[3]

And that's just thinking about the lucky ones with jobs. Unemployment and underemployment rates are extremely high among recent college graduates when compared to pre–Great Recession figures. In 2015, young degree holders had an unemployment rate of 7.2 percent and an underemployment rate of nearly 15 percent. In 2007, their unemployment rate was only 5.5 percent and underemployment rate was 9.6 percent.[4]

It should be no surprise then that one in four of Americans with student loan debt are either delinquent or in default. To add insult to injury, student loan debt is one of the most difficult of obligations to discharge in bankruptcy proceedings.[5]

Student loan debt is preventing millions of young grads from making investments, starting their own businesses, and pursuing other financial decisions that are necessary for reaching the American Dream. It is not healthy for our economy and our society to have this much student loan debt floating around.[6]

Student debt has become a major political issue in recent years, and one of the reasons Bernie Sanders was able to attract so much support among young people was due to his plan to make public college education free and his proposals to dramatically lower the interest rates of student loans and offering more assistance to help pay them off.[7]

Soaring student loan debt is caused by a couple of different factors. One is the large amount of loans students are taking out to finance their education at for-profit colleges. Another is the skyrocketing cost for tuition at all universities. One of the factors driving up tuition is the drastic expansion of college administrative positions.

ADMINISTRATIVE BLOAT

One thing universities are certainly not short on is administrators. Higher education is up to its neck in bureaucrats, from college deans to multicultural center chiefs. Over several decades, the number of administrators has increased greatly in comparison with the number of students and faculty. From 1987 to 2012, universities more than doubled the number of nonacademic professionals they employ with the addition of more than five hundred thousand administrators. In that same time frame, the cost for education, adjusted for inflation, doubled at private institutions and nearly tripled at public colleges.[8]

Explanations for such a massive increase in the college

bureaucracy center on the need to adjust to technological changes, demands from the federal government for schools to comply with stringent mandates, and unwillingness on the part of professors to serve in administrative roles. In an in-depth essay on administrative bloat, Johns Hopkins University political scientist Benjamin Ginsberg agreed that some of these reasons explain why colleges have more managers on their payroll, but not why they have so many. Ginsberg argues that the real reason for the expansion is the bureaucrats' desire to solidify their power and prestige through the expansion of the staff and budgets they oversee.

There are several consequences of this pursuit of petty power, according to the Johns Hopkins professor. One is that there is not enough work for these admins to do, so they usually participate in "make-work"—such as meetings on planning future meetings—all day. My own personal experience can support that claim, as the administrators I dealt with as a student always seemed to be either in frivolous meetings or enjoying two-hour lunch breaks. Other results of this expansion include corruption and an obsession with fund-raising for the sole purpose of lavishing spectacular pay raises and other amenities on administrators.[9]

When faced with accusations that they are the reason why college tuition is skyrocketing, administrators are quick to blame it on the elimination of state and federal subsidies instead. But that is not quite an accurate picture, according to University of Colorado law professor Paul Campos. In a *New York Times* op-ed, Campos asserted, "public investment in higher education in America is vastly larger today, in inflation-adjusted dollars, than it was during the supposed golden age of public funding in the 1960s." Moreover, it has grown at a faster rate than government spending as a whole.

Campos says it is more accurate to place the blame on college administrators and the prevalence of six- and seven-figure salaries among the top echelons of the academic bureaucracy for why Americans are spending more to get a degree.[10]

Compounding their financial baggage is the role administrators play in enabling campus insanity. The lower rungs of the bureaucratic ladder are employed specifically to promote such issues as diversity, gender equality, and other topics that align their interests with those of the agitators. The higher-ups seem to lack any trace of testicular fortitude and do everything possible to placate demonstrators. They are easily cowed into suppressing speech if it offends a protected class and are also assigned to handling campus rape allegations—a job they seem utterly incompetent at performing.

Administrators are not just useless—they're also harmful to a campus environment.

THE REVENUE SPORTS SHAM

Sports are an integral part of the modern-day college experience. And by sports, we are not talking about softball and rowing. The athletic competition that drives the most interest is the so-called revenue sports, which for most schools are football and men's basketball. They fill stadiums of crazed fans, draw lucrative TV rights contracts, and generate millions in merchandise sales. But they're also costing an arm and a leg to keep up. In 2015, spending increases on college sports exceeded the amount revenue increased from the previous year among Division I schools. According to the NCAA, only around twenty colleges can cover the costs of athletics without reaching into taxpayer money and student fees.

The "revenue" in revenue sports isn't actually cutting it for most schools, but the intense interest shown for college sports by students, alumni, and unaffiliated fans seems enough of a reason to keep the behemoth going. Experts see college sports as a bubble that could pop at any moment due to the skyrocketing expenses required to keep it at its current level.[11]

But the major problem with revenue sports might not be the financial costs, but the ethical quandaries that go hand in hand with them. Several college programs have been caught in recent years committing flagrant academic fraud in order to keep their valued "student-athletes" on the field. The most famous example is that of the University of North Carolina. A literacy counselor for UNC's athletic department, Mary Willingham, turned whistle-blower when she went public with the revelation that many of the university's star athletes were taking fake classes. As evidence of the fraud, she submitted a poorly written, paragraph-length essay that had received an A–. UNC officials did everything in their power to discredit and ignore the whistle-blower's allegations, but their own investigation in 2014 found that the athletic department had been engaged in this kind of academic fraud for nearly twenty years.[12]

A CNN investigation of several college athletic departments in the wake of the UNC scandal showed similar improprieties across the board, with many student-athletes demonstrating fifth-grade reading levels.[13] *Inside Higher Ed* reported that as of 2016, more than a dozen college athletic programs had been found guilty of academic fraud over the last decade. Considering the lengths to which UNC went to cover up its own fraud and deny a whistle-blower's account, it's likely that far more programs are engaged in this behavior than the ones unlucky enough to have been caught.

"It's an epidemic and a problem that will continue until faculty take control of their campuses," David Ridpath, a professor of sports administration at Ohio University, told *Inside Higher Ed* about the problem. "This can be changed, but we simply have to want to do it. This will not stop until we define what we are: professional sports being played in the higher ed space or a cocurricular activity played by students?"[14]

It is not just the athletes' bad grades that universities are covering up. Far more concerning is the willingness of coaches and administrators to hide the crimes of their top players. The most recent example of this egregious activity comes from Baylor University. During the eight-year tenure of head coach Art Briles, the man who made the school a football powerhouse, women who accused players of rape were repeatedly ignored or intimidated by school officials in order to safeguard the team's premier talent—even though two serial predators were on the team and the school nurse estimated that 25 to 50 percent of the rape victims she sees every year are assaulted by football players.[15] Multiple women have filed lawsuits against the school over the way it handled rape allegations, and Baylor fired Briles and demoted the university president due to their involvement in the affair.[16]

Baylor is certainly not alone in this behavior. The University of Tennessee forked over $2.48 million in 2016 to settle a rape lawsuit filed by eight women who accused the school of protecting football players they alleged assaulted them. All of the players implicated were found guilty of sexual assault by the school's own internal investigations but were allowed to remain on campus while the probes took place.[17] The one player who tried to help the women was called a traitor by head coach Butch Jones and beaten up by some of his fellow teammates.[18]

Numerous other schools—including the University of Oklahoma and the University of Missouri—have been caught turning the other way when it comes to the crimes of top athletic talent.[19]

It appears schools are willing to shoulder the financial burden of college sports, but are they willing to continue covering up the crimes and poor academics of their star players?

THE FAILURE TO EDUCATE

With the amount of money and time a college education requires, you would expect it to confer the necessary skills and knowledge to succeed in a competitive job market. Not so.

Recent studies are showing that the latest generation of college graduates is particularly ill prepared for work. Forty percent of graduates were found to lack the critical reasoning skills needed to do well in the workforce. Most employers rate college graduates as not having the skills necessary for employment.[20] Employers also believe that recent college graduates have poor writing skills and cannot communicate properly in a work environment. (As someone who has edited a substantial amount of intern writing, I concur with that assessment.) Strong communication skills are considered *the* top priority by many companies, and 80 percent of employers believe universities should do more to teach these skills to students.

However, all the blame might not be on colleges, as only 24 percent of high school seniors have proficient writing skills.[21]

Colleges have a plethora of problems, but the most damning

issue on its worth comes down to one question: Is it really worth taking on five figures of debt to attain an "education" that doesn't teach you anything of use?

NOTES

INTRODUCTION

1. Robby Soave, "Emory University President Vows to Hunt Down Student Whose 'Trump 2016' Message Wrecked Safe Space." *Hit & Run* (Reason.com blog), March 23, 2016, http://reason.com/blog/2016/03/23/emory-university-president-vows-to-hunt.

2. Ben Kew, "'Stop Islam,' Pro-Trump Messages Chalked onto University of Michigan Campus." *Breitbart News*, April 1, 2016, http://www.breitbart.com/tech/2016/04/01/stop-islam-pro-trump-messages-chalked-onto-university-of-michigan-campus/.

3. Scott Greer, "Student Government at Public University Wants to Kick Out Member over Pro-Trump Chalking," *Daily Caller*. April 6, 2016, http://dailycaller.com/2016/04/06/student-government-at-public-university-kicks-out-member-over-pro-trump-chalking/.

4. Scott Greer, "Student Leaders at Ohio University Condemn Trump Drawing as Racially Offensive," *Daily Caller*, April 11, 2016, http://dailycaller.com/2016/04/11/student-leaders-at-ohio-university-condemn-campus-trump-drawing-as-racially-offensive/.

5. Wilborn P. Nobles III, "'Trump Wall' at Kappa Alpha Fraternity Sets Tulane Abuzz," *NOLA.com* (blog). April 13, 2016, http://www.nola.com/education/index.ssf/2016/04/tulane_kappa_alpha_trump_wall.html.

6. Anthony Gockowski,. "DePaul Says No More Political Chalking in Response to Pro-Trump Messages," *Campus Reform*, April 12, 2016, http://campusreform.org/?ID=7483.

7. Scott Greer, "The Revolution Devours Its College Administrators," *Daily Caller*, November 13, 2015, http://dailycaller.com/2015/11/13/the-revolution-devours-its-college-administrators/; Eric Owens, "SURPRISE! Mizzou Sees Application Drop after Days of Protests, Illusory Klan Hoods, Poop Swastika," *Daily Caller*, January 8, 2016, http://dailycaller.com/2016/01/08/mizzou-sees-application-drop-after-days-of-protests-illusory-klan-hoods-poop-swastika/.

8. Nick Gass, "Bloomberg Booed as He Rips College 'Safe Spaces,'" *Politico*, May 2, 2016, http://www.politico.com/story/2016/05/michael-bloomberg-booed-michigan-commencement-222691.

9. Claire Landsbaum, "Bill Maher Goes Off on College Protesters: 'Who Raised These Little Monsters?'" *Complex,* November 14, 2015, http://www.complex.com/pop-culture/2015/11/bill-maher-goes-off-on-college-protesters-who-raised-these-little-monsters.

10. Thomas Sowell, "The University of Chicago Stands Athwart PC Madness," *National Review,* August 31, 2016, http://www.nationalreview.com/article/439519/university-chicago-safe-spaces-risk-loss-academic-freedom.

11. Kyle Feldscher, "Obama Tells Howard Grads to Vote, Ditch 'Safe Space' Culture," *Washington Examiner,* May 7, 2016, http://www.washingtonexaminer.com/obama-tells-howard-grads-to-vote-ditch-safe-space-culture/article/2590697.

12. Glenn Harlan Reynolds, "Glenn Reynolds: After Yale, Mizzou, Raise the Voting Age," *USA Today,* November 16, 2015, http://www.usatoday.com/story/opinion/2015/11/11/raise-voting-age-25-yale-missouri-protests-political-debate-column/75577468/.

13. Breitbart Tech, "No Punishment for Black Lives Matter Protesters Harassing Dartmouth Students," *Breitbart News,* May 31, 2016, http://www.breitbart.com/tech/2016/05/31/no-punishment-for-black-lives-matter-protesters-harrassing-dartmouth-students/.

14. Megan Dollar, "Despite MU's Decline in Enrollment, Other Missouri Universities See Increase," *The ManEater,* August 1, 2016, http://www.themaneater.com/stories/2016/8/1/despite-mus-decline-enrollment-other-missouri-univ/.

CHAPTER 1: CULT OF DIVERSITY

1. Exec. Order No. 10925 (1961).

2. "A Brief History of Affirmative Action," UCI Office of Equal Opportunity and Diversity, accessed September 13, 2016, http://www.oeod.uci.edu/aa.html.

3. Ahmed Younies, "Affirmative Action Laws Now Protect LGBT Employees of Federal Contractors," HR Unlimited Inc. blog, December 5, 2014, http://www.hrunlimitedinc.com/affirmative-action-laws-now-protect-lgbt-employees-of-federal-contractors/.

4. Brief Amicus Curia for Richard Sander in Support of Neither Party, *Fisher v. University of Texas,* No. 14-981. September 10, 2015, http://www.scotusblog.com/wp-content/uploads/2015/09/Sander-brief-for-Fisher-v-Univesrity-of-Texas-corrected.pdf.

5. Russell Cobb, "Why Do So Many People Pretend to Be Native American?" *Longreads* (blog), August 2014, https://blog.longreads.com/2014/08/04/why-do-people-continue-to-fashion-native-identities-out-of-thin-air/.

6. William Jacobson, "Trump Is Right about Elizabeth Warren's Native American Problem," *Legal Insurrection* (blog), May 6, 2016, http://legalinsurrection.com/2016/05/trump-is-right-about-elizabeth-warrens-native-american-problem/.

7. Rebecca Hawkes, "Mindy Kaling's Brother 'Pretended to Be Black' to Get into Medical School," *Telegraph* (UK), April 6, 2015, http://www.telegraph.co.uk/culture/books/booknews/11517877/Mindy-Kalings-brother-pretended-to-be-black-to-get-into-medical-school.html.

8. *Merriam-Webster's Learner's Dictionary*, s.v. "diversity," accessed October 10, 2016, http://www.merriam-webster.com/dictionary/diversity.

9. Lewis F. Powell Jr., "Regents of the Univ. of Cal. v. Bakke," Legal Information Institute, June 28, 1978, https://www.law.cornell.edu/supremecourt/text/438/265.

10. Sandra Day O'Connor, "Grutter v. Bollinger," Legal Information Institute, June 23, 2003, https://www.law.cornell.edu/supct/html/02-241.ZO.html.

11. William Rhenquist, "Gratz v. Bollinger," Legal Information Institute, June 23, 2003, https://www.law.cornell.edu/supct/html/02-516.ZO.html.

12. Peter Schmidt, "Sandra Day O'Connor Revisits and Revives Affirmative-Action Controversy," *Chronicle of Higher Education*, January 14, 2010, http://www.chronicle.com/article/sandra-day-oconnor-revisits/63523.

13. Lee Bollinger, "Seven Myths about Affirmative Action in Universities," Columbia University in the City of New York, 2002, accessed September 13, 2016, http://www.columbia.edu/node/8321.html.

14. Lee Bollinger, "Office of the President Lee C. Bollinger: Why Diversity Matters," Columbia University in the City of New York, June 1, 2007, http://www.columbia.edu/cu/president/docs/communications/2006-2007/070601-why-diversity-matters-chronicle.html.

15. Bradford Richardson, "Yale Students: Studying White, Male Writers Creates Culture 'Hostile to Students of Color,'" Washington Times, June 2, 2016, http://www.washingtontimes.com/news/2016/jun/2/yale-students-white-male-writers-hostile-culture/.

16. Brief of General Motors Corporation as Amicus Curiae in Support of Appellants, *Grutter v. Bollinger*, No. 01-1447, May 30, 2001, https://diversity.umich.edu/admissions/legal/gru_amicus/gru_gm.html.

17. Roger Parloff, "Big Business Asks Supreme Court to Save Affirmative Action," *Fortune*, December 9, 2015, http://fortune.com/2015/12/09/supreme-court-affirmative-action/.

18. Sheen S. Levine and David Stark, "Diversity Makes You Brighter," *New York Times*, December 9, 2015, http://www.nytimes.com/2015/12/09/opinion/diversity-makes-you-brighter.html?action=click.

19. Robert D Putnam, "*E Pluribus Unum*: Diversity and Community in the Twenty-First Century: The 2006 Johan Skytte Prize Lecture," *Scandinavian Political Studies* 30, no. 2 (June 2007): 137–74.

20. "Political Scientist: Does Diversity Really Work?" NPR, August 15, 2007, http://www.npr.org/templates/story/story.php?storyId=12802663.

21. Frank Dobbin and Alexandra Kalev, "Why Diversity Programs Fail," *Harvard Business Review*, August 2016, https://hbr.org/2016/07/why-diversity-programs-fail.

22. Shimshock, Rob. "Survey: Dartmouth Students Prefer Nonwhite Faculty, Classmates." *Campus Reform.* July 6, 2016. Accessed September 13, 2016. http://www.campusreform. org/?ID=7806.

23. "Dartmouth Class of 2019 Profile," Dartmouth University, accessed September 13, 2016, https://admissions.dartmouth.edu/facts-advice/facts/class-profile.

24. Peter Fricke, "Students Plan Walkout to Protest Cuts to UT Diversity and Inclusion Office," *Campus Reform*, April 19, 2016, http://www.campusreform.org/?ID=7504.

25. Blake Neff, "Public College Drops Math Requirement, May Replace It with Diversity," *Daily Caller*, June 14, 2016, http://dailycaller.com/2016/06/14/public-college-drops-math-requirement-may-replace-it-with-diversity/.

26. William Nardi, "Public University Now Requires Applicants Pledge Commitment to 'Diversity and Inclusion,'" the College Fix, July 11, 2016, http://www.thecollegefix.com/post/28105/.

27. James Webb, "Diversity and the Myth of White Privilege," *Wall Street Journal*, July 22, 2010, http://www.wsj.com/articles/SB10001424052748703724104575379630952309 408.

28. Ron Unz, "The Myth of American Meritocracy," *American Conservative*, November 28, 2012, http://www.theamericanconservative.com/articles/the-myth-of-american-meritocracy/.

29. Douglas Belkin, "Asian-American Groups Seek Investigation into Ivy League Admissions," *Wall Street Journal,* May 23, 2016, http://www.wsj.com/articles/asian-american-groups-seek-investigation-into-ivy-league-admissions-1464026150.

30. Richard Sander and Stuart Taylor Jr., "The Painful Truth about Affirmative Action," *Atlantic*, October 2, 2012, http://www.theatlantic.com/national/archive/2012/10/the-painful-truth-about-affirmative-action/263122/.

31. Anemona Hartocollis, "With Remarks in Affirmative Action Case, Scalia Steps into 'Mismatch' Debate," *New York Times*, December 10, 2015, http://www.nytimes. com/2015/12/11/us/with-remarks-in-affirmative-action-case-scalia-steps-into-mismatch-debate.html?_r=0.

CHAPTER 2: POLITICAL CORRECTNESS IN THE AGE OF MICROAGGRESSIONS

1. Robert D McFadden, "Political Correctness: New Bias Test?" *New York Times,* May 5, 1991, http://www.nytimes.com/1991/05/05/us/political-correctness-new-bias-test.html.

2. Richard Bernstein. "In Dispute on Bias, Stanford Is Likely To Alter Western Culture Program." *The New York Times.* January 19, 1988. http://www.nytimes. com/1988/01/19/us/in-dispute-on-bias-stanford-is-likely-to-alter-western-culture-program.html?pagewanted=all.

3. Michael Lind, "Western Civ Fights Back," *New York Times*, September 6, 1998, http:// www.nytimes.com/1998/09/06/books/western-civ-fights-back.html.

4. "Court Overturns Stanford University Code Barring Bigoted Speech." *New York Times*, March 1, 1995, http://www.nytimes.com/1995/03/01/us/court-overturns-stanford-university-code-barring-bigoted-speech.html.

5. Jacob Poushter, "40% of Millennials OK with Limiting Speech Offensive to Minorities," Pew Research Center Fact Tank, November 20, 2015, http://www.pewresearch.org/fact-tank/2015/11/20/40-of-millennials-ok-with-limiting-speech-offensive-to-minorities/.

6. "Dickinson College Bias Incident Protocol," accessed October 10, 2016, https://www.dickinson.edu/download/downloads/id/4882/bias_incident_protocol_2015pdf.pdf.

7. FIRE, "Spotlight on Speech Codes 2016," Foundation for Individual Rights in Education, accessed September 14, 2016, https://www.thefire.org/spotlight-on-speech-codes-2016/.

8. Robby Soave, "College Disciplines Students—One Black, One White—For Racial Joke," *Daily Caller*, April 28, 2014, http://dailycaller.com/2014/04/28/college-disciplines-students-one-black-one-white-for-racial-joke/.

9. Robby Soave, "Colorado College Suspends Student for 2 Years. His Crime? Telling a Stupid Joke." *Hit & Run* (blog), December 7, 2015, http://reason.com/blog/2015/12/07/colorado-college-suspends-student-for-2.

10. Derald Wing Sue, "Racial Microaggressions in Everyday Life," *Psychology Today*, October 2, 2010, https://www.psychologytoday.com/blog/microaggressions-in-everyday-life/201010/racial-microaggressions-in-everyday-life.

11. Stephanie Saul, "Campuses Cautiously Train Freshmen Against Subtle Insults," *New York Times*, September 6, 2016, http://www.nytimes.com/2016/09/07/us/campuses-cautiously-train-freshmen-against-subtle-insults.html.

12. Peter Hasson, "'Inclusive Terminology' Guide at University of Missouri Raises Awareness of 'Adultism,'" *Daily Caller*, December 19, 2015, http://dailycaller.com/2015/12/19/inclusive-terminology-guide-at-university-of-missouri-raises-awareness-of-adultism/.

13. Katherine Timpf, "U of Wisconsin Faculty Advised Not to Say 'America Is a Melting Pot' Because That's Racist." *National Review*. July 1, 2015. Accessed September 14, 2016. http://www.nationalreview.com/article/420619/u-wisconsin-faculty-advised-not-say-america-melting-pot-because-thats-racist.

14. Josh Hedtke, "California Professors Instructed Not to Say 'America Is the Land of Opportunity,'" College Fix, June 10, 2015, http://www.thecollegefix.com/post/22839/.

15. Stacey Anne Hartwood et al., *Racial Microaggressions @ University of Illinois, Urbana-Champaign* (University of Illinois at Urbana-Champaign, 2015), 6, http://www.racialmicroaggressions.illinois.edu/files/2015/03/RMA-Classroom-Report.pdf.

16. Eric Owens, "Public University's Bias-Free Language Guide Calls the Word 'American' 'PROBLEMATIC,'" *Daily Caller*, July 28, 2015, http://dailycaller.com/2015/07/28/public-universitys-bias-free-language-guide-calls-the-word-american-problematic/.

17. "Report Details Microaggressions on Campuses for Students of Color and Women," Inside Higher Ed, accessed September 14, 2016, https://www.insidehighered.com/news/2015/01/08/report-details-microaggressions-campuses-students-color-and-women.

18. Scott Greer, "Orwell's Newspeak Is Coming to a Campus Near You," *Daily Caller*, August 29, 2015, http://dailycaller.com/2015/08/29/orwells-newspeak-is-coming-to-a-campus-near-you/.

19. Steven Elbow, "UW Student's 'Rape Culture' Letter Draws Outrage," *Cap Times* (Madison, WI), November 5, 2013, http://host.madison.com/ct/news/local/writers/steven_elbow/uw-student-s-rape-culture-letter-draws-outrage/article_bdb3f2ae-2515-5333-aeb0-3614757caed7.html.

20. Greg Piper, "'Michigan Daily': We Fired Columnist Because He Mocked Our 'Experiences,'" College Fix, December 18, 2014, http://www.thecollegefix.com/post/20542/.

21. Kaitlyn Schallhorn, "College Newspaper Loses Thousands in Funding after Publishing Negative Black Lives Matter Op-Ed." *TheBlaze*, October 20, 2015, http://www.theblaze.com/stories/2015/10/20/college-newspaper-loses-thousands-in-funding-after-publishing-negative-black-lives-matter-editorial/.

22. Tré Goins-Phillips, "Professor Claims 'Neo-Nazi' Ben Shapiro's Campus Lecture Left Students 'Brutalized,'" *TheBlaze*, May 26, 2016, http://www.theblaze.com/stories/2016/05/26/professor-claims-neo-nazi-ben-shapiros-campus-lecture-left-students-brutalized/.

23. Blake Neff, "VIDEO: DePaul University Descends into Chaos over Milo Yiannopoulos Visit," *Daily Caller*, May 24, 2016, http://dailycaller.com/2016/05/24/video-depaul-university-descends-into-chaos-over-milo-yiannopoulos-visit/.

24. Dennis Holtschneider, "Tuesday's Speech and Protest," DePaul University, May 25, 2016, http://offices.depaul.edu/president/speeches-and-communications/2015-16/Pages/Tuesday-speech-and-protest.aspx.

25. Jamie Altman, "DePaul President Announces Resignation during Period of Campus Unrest," *USA Today*, June 15, 2016, http://college.usatoday.com/2016/06/15/depaul-president-announces-resignation-during-period-of-campus-unrest/.

26. Amber Athey, "DePaul Bans Ben Shapiro," Campus Reform, August 1, 2016, http://www.campusreform.org/?ID=7923.

27. Scott Greer, "The Left's Outrage at Jerry Seinfeld Proves His Point," *Daily Caller*, June 13, 2015, http://dailycaller.com/2015/06/13/the-lefts-outrage-at-jerry-seinfeld-proves-his-point/.

28. "What Is a Safe Space?" Safe Space Network, accessed September 21, 2016, http://safespacenetwork.tumblr.com/Safespace.

29. Eric Owens, "Militant Georgetown Feminists Demand 'SAFE SPACE' Because of Scary 5'5", 130-Lb. Woman," *Daily Caller*, April 20, 2015, http://dailycaller.com/2015/04/20/georgetown-feminists-demand-safe-space-because-of-conservative-lecturer/.

30. Judith Shulevitz, "In College and Hiding from Scary Ideas," *New York Times*, March 21, 2015, http://www.nytimes.com/2015/03/22/opinion/sunday/judith-shulevitz-hiding-from-scary-ideas.html?_r=0.

31. Eric Owens, "Meet Mizzou Professor Who Threatened Reporter With MOB ATTACK," *Daily Caller*, November 9, 2015, http://dailycaller.com/2015/11/09/meet-the-sick-mizzou-media-professor-who-threatened-a-reporter-with-mob-violence-video/.

32. Michael Miller, "Columbia Students Claim Greek Mythology Needs a Trigger Warning," *Washington Post*, May 14, 2015, https://www.washingtonpost.com/news/morning-mix/wp/2015/05/14/columbia-students-claim-greek-mythology-needs-a-trigger-warning/.

33. Judith Shulevitz, "In College and Hiding from Scary Ideas," *New York Times*, March 21, 2015, http://www.nytimes.com/2015/03/22/opinion/sunday/judith-shulevitz-hiding-from-scary-ideas.html?_r=0.

34. Greg Lukianoff and Jonathan Haidt, "The Coddling of the American Mind," *Atlantic*, September 2015, http://www.theatlantic.com/magazine/archive/2015/09/the-coddling-of-the-american-mind/399356/.

35. Ibid.

36. Eric Posner, "Colleges Need Speech Codes Because Their Students Are Still Children," *Slate*, February 12, 2015, http://www.slate.com/articles/news_and_politics/view_from_chicago/2015/02/university_speech_codes_students_are_children_who_must_be_protected.html.

37. Jonathan Chait, "Not a Very P.C. Thing to Say," *New York*, January 27, 2015, http://nymag.com/daily/intelligencer/2015/01/not-a-very-pc-thing-to-say.html.

38. Herbert Marcuse, "Repressive Tolerance," in *A Critique of Pure Tolerance* (Boston: Beacon Press, 1969), 95–137.

CHAPTER 3: VICTIMHOOD CULTURE

1. Bradley Campbell and Jason Manning, "Microaggression and Moral Culture," *Comparative Sociology* 13, no. 6 (January 2014): 692–726, doi:10.1163/15691330-12341332.

2. Ibid., 710.

3. Ibid., 713.

4. Ibid., 721–23.

5. Ibid., 724–25

6. R. Kurt Osenlund, "Sinful Cinema: Ace Ventura: Pet Detective, the Most Offensive and Homophobic Football Movie Ever Made," *The House Next Door* (*Slant* magazine blog), January 31, 2014, http://www.slantmagazine.com/house/article/sinful-cinema-ace-ventura-pet-detective-the-most-offensive-and-homophobic-football-movie-ever-made.

7. Betsy Rothstein, "ACLU Goes Full Fascist, Tells People Which Pronouns to Use for Man-Parted Caitlyn Jenner," *Daily Caller*, June 2, 2015, http://dailycaller.com/2015/06/02/aclu-goes-full-fascist-tells-people-which-pronouns-to-use-for-penis-laden-caitlyn-jenner/.

8. Blake Neff, "Students Demand Gay Activist Movie Be Cancelled for Being Too White, Gay," *Daily Caller*, November 4, 2015, http://dailycaller.com/2015/11/04/students-demand-gay-activist-movie-be-cancelled-for-being-too-white-gay/.

9. Austin Ruse, "Lesbian Legend Scoffs at Transgender Men, Gets Fired by Gay Group," *Breitbart*, May 2, 2016, http://www.breitbart.com/big-government/2016/05/02/lesbian-legend-fired-parade-scoffing-transgender/.

10. Mathew Rodriguez, "Feminist Germaine Greer Doubles down on Anti-Trans Rhetoric in New Interview," Mic, December 4, 2015, https://mic.com/articles/129699/feminist-germaine-greer-doubles-down-on-anti-trans-rhetoric-in-new-interview.

11. Elinor Burkett, "What Makes a Woman?" *New York Times*, June 6, 2015, http://www.nytimes.com/2015/06/07/opinion/sunday/what-makes-a-woman.html?_r=0.

12. Paul McHugh, "Transgender Surgery Isn't the Solution," *Wall Street Journal*, March 13, 2016, http://www.wsj.com/articles/paul-mchugh-transgender-surgery-isnt-the-solution-1402615120.

13. Lawrence S. Mayer and Paul R. McHugh, "Sexuality and Gender: Findings from the Biological, Psychological, and Social Sciences," *New Atlantis: A Journal of Technology and Society*, no. 50 (Fall 2016): 7–9.

14. Friedrich Wilhelm Nietzsche, "Beyond Good and Evil," *Basic Writings of Nietzsche*, trans. Walter Arnold Kaufmann (New York: Modern Library, 2000), 391–97.

15. Ibid.

16. Ibid.

17. Nietzsche , "On the Genealogy of Morals," in ibid., 460–73.

18. Friedrich Wilhelm Nietzsche, *The Will to Power*, ed. Walter Arnold Kaufmann (New York: Random House, 1967).

19. Ibid., 482.

20. Jonah Goldberg, "Empty Integrity," *National Review*, November 10, 2014, http://www.nationalreview.com/article/392395/empty-integrity-jonah-goldberg.

21. Allan Bloom, *The Closing of the American Mind: How Higher Education Has Failed Democracy and Impoverished the Souls of Today's Students* (New York: Simon and Schuster, 1987).

22. Paul Gottfried, "Understanding Nietzsche," *First Principles*, February 2, 2009, http://www.firstprinciplesjournal.com/print.aspx?article=1211.

23. Jonah Goldberg, "The Nietzschean Concept That Explains Today's PC Culture," *National Review*, June 19, 2015, http://www.nationalreview.com/article/420010/nietzschean-concept-explains-todays-pc-culture-jonah-goldberg.

CHAPTER 4: IDENTITY POLITICS

1. Tasneem Nashrulla, "'Welcome White Week' Flyer at a Kentucky University Sparks Student Protest," *Buzzfeed*, September 7, 2016, https://www.buzzfeed.com/tasneemnashrulla/welcome-white-week-flyer-kentucky-university?utm_term=.uqAgdkrGa#.iqDRxe10y.

2. Allum Bokhari, "The Media Is Wrong. White Student Unions Are Not 'Hoaxes' Created by Racists," Breitbart News, November 24, 2015, http://www.breitbart.com/tech/2015/11/24/exclusive-the-media-is-wrong-white-student-unions-are-not-hoaxes-created-by-racists/.

3. Carl Schmitt, *The Concept of the Political*, exp. ed., trans. George Schwab (Chicago: University of Chicago Press, 2007), 26–27.

4. Conor Friedersdorf, "The Perils of Writing a Provocative Email at Yale," *Atlantic*, May 26, 2016, http://www.theatlantic.com/politics/archive/2016/05/the-peril-of-writing-a-provocative-email-at-yale/484418/.

5. Daniel Mael, "On Many Campuses, Hate Is Spelled SJP," *Tower* magazine, October 2014, http://www.thetower.org/article/on-many-campuses-hate-is-spelled-sjp/; Jake New, "Jews Need Not Apply?" Inside Higher Ed, March 3, 2015, https://www.insidehighered.com/news/2015/03/03/ucla-student-government-questions-judicial-board-nominee-being-jewish.

6. Anthony Berteaux, "In the Safe Spaces on Campus, No Jews Allowed," *Tower*, February 2016, http://www.thetower.org/article/in-the-safe-spaces-on-campus-no-jews-allowed/.

7. Kellan Howell, "Saida Grundy, Boston University Professor: White Males a 'Problem Population,'" *Washington Times,* May 9, 2015, http://www.washingtontimes.com/news/2015/may/9/saida-grundy-boston-university-professor-white-mal/.

8. Scott Greer, "Dear Paul Ryan: America Was Actually Founded on an Identity," *Daily Caller*, March 24, 2016, http://dailycaller.com/2016/03/24/dear-paul-ryan-america-was-actually-founded-on-an-identity/.

9. Gunnar Myrdal, *An American Dilemma: The Negro Problem and Modern Democracy* (New York: Harper & Row, 1962).

10. Samuel P. Huntington, *Who Are We? The Challenges to America's National Identity* (New York: Simon & Schuster, 2004).

11. Nicholas Pappas, "Missouri Students: Thomas Jefferson a 'Racist Rapist,' Campus Statue Needs to Go," *Daily Caller*, October 13, 2015, http://dailycaller.com/2015/10/13/missouri-students-thomas-jefferson-a-racist-rapist-campus-statue-needs-to-go/.

12. Scott Jaschik, "Thomas Jefferson Is Next Target of Students Who Question Honors for Figures Who Were Racists," *Inside Higher Ed*, November 23, 2015, https://www.insidehighered.com/news/2015/11/23/thomas-jefferson-next-target-students-who-question-honors-figures-who-were-racists.

13. Blake Neff, "Profs Demand University President Stop Quoting Thomas Jefferson At His Own School," *Daily Caller*, November 14, 2016, http://dailycaller.com/2016/11/14/profs-demand-university-president-stop-quoting-thomas-jefferson-at-his-own-school/#ixzz4QmPD1Ws1.

14. Scott Greer, "The Guy Who Founded America Is No Longer Welcome at Democratic Dinner Tables," *Daily Caller*, July 24, 2015, http://dailycaller.com/2015/07/24/the-guy-who-founded-america-is-no-longer-welcome-at-democrat-dinner-tables/.

15. Nick Allen, "Yale University to Consider Renaming College Honouring John C. Calhoun, a Slavery Supporter," *Telegraph*, August 1, 2016, http://www.telegraph.co.uk/news/2016/08/01/yale-university-to-consider-renaming-college-honouring-john-c-ca/.

16. Gabriel Fisher, "Princeton and the Fight over Woodrow Wilson's Legacy," *New Yorker*, November 25, 2015, http://www.newyorker.com/news/news-desk/princeton-and-the-fight-over-woodrow-wilsons-legacy.

17. Bradford Richardson, "Yale Students: Studying White, Male Writers Creates Culture 'Hostile to Students of Color,'" *Washington Times*, June 2, 2016, http://www.washingtontimes.com/news/2016/jun/2/yale-students-white-male-writers-hostile-culture/.

18. "The Philosophy of MEChA," National MEChA, accessed September 12, 2016, http://www.nationalmecha.org/philosophy.html.

19. Charlie Norwood, "Exclusive: The Truth about 'La Raza,'" *Human Events*, April 7, 2006, http://humanevents.com/2006/04/07/emexclusive-emthe-truth-about-la-raza/.

CHAPTER 5: GUILTY OF BEING WHITE

1. Sarah Dutton et al., "Negative Views of Race Relations Reach All-Time High— CBS/NYT Poll," CBS News, July 13, 2016, http://www.cbsnews.com/news/negative-views-of-race-relations-reach-all-time-high-cbsnyt-poll/.

2. Susan Sontag, "What's Happening to America? (A Symposium)." *Partisan Review*, 1967, 57–58.

3. Amber Randall, "Georgetown Makes Students Do Walk of Shame to Atone for Slavery," *Daily Caller*, September 2, 2016, http://dailycaller.com/2016/09/02/georgetown-makes-students-do-walk-of-shame-to-atone-for-slavery/.

4. "Georgetown University Works to Amend Involvement in Slavery," NPR, September 2, 2016, http://www.npr.org/2016/09/02/492443229/georgetown-university-works-to-amend-involvement-in-slavery.

5. George Yancy, "Dear White America," *New York Times*, December 24, 2015, http://opinionator.blogs.nytimes.com/2015/12/24/dear-white-america/?_r=0.

6. Benjamin Wallace Wells, "The Hard Truths of Ta-Nehisi Coates," *New York Magazine*, July 12, 2015, http://nymag.com/daily/intelligencer/2015/07/ta-nehisi-coates-between-the-world-and-me.html.

7. H. Rambsy, "Coverage of Ta-Nehisi Coates and Between the World and Me," *Cultural Front*, June 26, 2015, http://www.culturalfront.org/2015/06/coverage-of-ta-nehisi-coates-and.html.

8. Ta-Nehisi Coates, *Between the World and Me* (New York: Spiegel & Grau, 2015), 86–87.

9. Diane Toroian Keaggy, "First Year Reading Program Selects 'Between the World and Me,'" The Source, May 9, 2016, https://source.wustl.edu/2016/05/first-year-reading-program-selects-world/.

10. Felice León, "Ta-Nehisi Coates on Why Whites Like His Writing," *Daily Beast*, October 25, 2015, http://www.thedailybeast.com/articles/2015/10/25/why-do-white-people-love-ta-nehisi-coates-work.html.

11. Ta-Nehisi Coates, "The Case for Reparations," *Atlantic*, June 2014, http://www.theatlantic.com/magazine/archive/2014/06/the-case-for-reparations/361631/.

12. Ibid.

13. Ibid.

14. Susan Svrluga, "Descendants of Slaves Sold by Georgetown Call for a $1 Billion Foundation for 'Reconciliation,'" *Washington Post*, September 8, 2016, https://www.washingtonpost.com/news/grade-point/wp/2016/09/08/descendants-of-slaves-sold-by-georgetown-call-for-a-1-billion-foundation-for-reconciliation/.

15. Jennifer Gould and Lorena Mongelli, "Ta-Nehisi Coates Selling Brooklyn Brownstone over Safety Concerns," *New York Post*, May 31, 2016, http://nypost.com/2016/05/31/writer-ta-nehisi-coates-selling-2m-brooklyn-brownstone-over-safety-concerns/.

16. "Hillary Clinton: 'We White Americans . . . Need to Recognize Our Privilege,'" NBC News, July 18, 2016, http://www.nbcnews.com/video/hillary-clinton-we-white-americans-need-to-recognize-our-privilege-727176259735.

17. McIntosh, Peggy. "White Privilege: Unpacking the Invisible Backpack." USDC.edu. Accessed September 12, 2016. http://code.ucsd.edu/pcosman/Backpack.pdfhttp://code.ucsd.edu/pcosman/Backpack.pdf.

18. "Glossary for Understanding the Dismantling Structural Racism/Promoting Racial Equity Analysis," Aspen Institute, https://assets.aspeninstitute.org/content/uploads/files/content/docs/rcc/RCC-Structural-Racism-Glossary.pdf.

19. Heather Mac Donald, "The Myth of Criminal-Justice Racism," *City Journal*, October 23, 2015, http://www.city-journal.org/html/myth-criminal-justice-racism-10231.html.

20. Robby Soave, "Activists to UMich: Admit Unqualified Students, If They Are Black," *Daily Caller*, April 16, 2014, http://dailycaller.com/2014/04/16/activists-to-umich-admit-unqualified-students-if-they-are-black/.

21. Robby Soave, "UMich Meets Demands of Black Students Who Threatened 'Physical Action,'" *Daily Caller*, January 27, 2014, http://dailycaller.com/2014/01/27/umich-meets-demands-of-black-students-who-threatened-physical-action/#ixzz2z5EWGQFE.

22. Lee Stranahan, "Video Shows University of Missouri Activist Jonathan Butler Falsified Key Claim Against President," *Breitbart*, November 11, 2015, http://www.breitbart.com/big-government/2015/11/11/video-shows-university-missouri-activist-jonathan-butler-falsified-key-claim-president/.

23. Eric Owens, "Mizzou Football Players ON STRIKE over Racism Claims," *Daily Caller*, November 8, 2015, http://dailycaller.com/2015/11/08/university-of-missouri-football-players-boycott-football-over-black-activists-hunger-strike/.

24. Brad Crawford, "Here's the List of Demands from Mizzou's Protesting Athletes, Students," *Saturday Down South*, November 8, 2015, http://www.saturdaydownsouth.com/mizzou-football/heres-list-demands-mizzous-protesting-athletes-students/.

25. Jillian Frankel, "Afrikan Student Union Releases Demands for UCLA Administration," *Daily Bruin*, October 26, 2015, http://dailybruin.com/2015/10/26/afrikan-student-union-releases-demands-for-ucla-administration/.

26. "ASU Disappointed in Block, Plans to Push UCLA to Address All Demands," *Daily Bruin*, November 14, 2015, http://dailybruin.com/2015/11/14/asu-disappointed-in-block-plans-to-push-ucla-to-address-all-demands/.

27. Jeremy Beaman, "Cal State LA Offers Segregated Housing for Black Students," College Fix, September 6, 2016, http://www.thecollegefix.com/post/28906/.

28. Eric Owens, "White University of Kansas Guy Now on Racial Hunger Strike," *Daily Caller*, November 16, 2015, http://dailycaller.com/2015/11/16/white-university-of-kansas-guy-now-on-racial-hunger-strike/.

29. Arielle Clay, "UNC-CH Students Interrupt Town Hall Meeting with List of Demands," WRAL, November 19, 2015, http://www.wral.com/unc-ch-students-interrupt-town-hall-meeting-with-list-of-demands-/15121491/.

30. "Campus Demands," The Demands, December 8, 2015, http://www.thedemands.org/.

31. "Our Demands," Black Liberation Collective, accessed September 8, 2016, http://www.blackliberationcollective.org/our-demands/.

32. "Our Principles," Black Liberation Collective, accessed September 8, 2016, http://www.blackliberationcollective.org/our-beliefs/.

33. Blake Neff, "Dartmouth Admin APOLOGIZES to Protesters Who Menaced Students," *Daily Caller*, November 17, 2015, http://dailycaller.com/2015/11/17/dartmouth-admin-apologizes-to-protesters-who-menaced-students/.

34. Blake Neff, "Mizzou Protesters Now Segregating Their Members by Race," *Daily Caller*, November 11, 2015, http://dailycaller.com/2015/11/11/mizzou-protesters-now-segregating-their-members-by-race/.

35. Peter Hasson, "Report: Vanderbilt Football Rape Was Payback for '400 Years of Slavery,'" *Daily Caller*, July 18, 2016, http://dailycaller.com/2016/07/18/report-vanderbilt-football-rape-was-payback-for-400-years-of-slavery/.

36. Peter Hasson, "Universities Are Singling-Out White Students for 'Education Sessions,'" *Daily Caller*, April 13, 2016, http://dailycaller.com/2016/04/13/universities-are-singling-out-white-students-for-education-sessions/.

37. Kaitlyn Schallhorn, "University Calls the Amount of White People on Campus a 'Failure,' Asks for Ideas on How to Have Fewer," *Campus Reform*, April 15, 2014, http://campusreform.org/?ID=5549.

38. Carly Rolph, "Student-Activists Release List of Extreme Social Justice-Based Demands," *Daily Caller*, March 7, 2016, http://dailycaller.com/2016/03/07/student-activists-release-list-of-extreme-social-justice-based-demands/.

39. Howard Hecht, "#StopWhitePeople2K16" Is an Official Part of Residential Assistant Training," *Binghamton Review*, August 21, 2016, http://www.binghamtonreview.com/2016/08/stopwhitepeople2k16-is-an-official-part-of-residential-assistant-training/.

40. "University Responds to Criticism over '#StopWhitePeople2K16' Training Course," CBS News, August 25, 2016, http://www.cbsnews.com/news/binghamton-university-responds-criticism-over-stopwhitepeople2k16-training-course/.

41. Steven Glick, "Pomona College Poster: 'Everyone Is Problematic,'" *Claremont Independent*, September 6, 2016, http://claremontindependent.com/pomona-college-poster-everyone-is-problematic/.

42. Steven Glick, "Safe Spaces Segregate the Claremont Colleges," *Claremont Independent*, November 17, 2015, http://claremontindependent.com/safe-spaces-segregate-the-claremont-colleges/.

43. Eric Owens,. "Mizzou Freshman Orientation: Black Lives Matter Protesters Are HEROES," *Daily Caller*, July 8, 2016, http://dailycaller.com/2016/07/08/mizzou-freshman-orientation-paints-black-lives-matter-protesters-as-civil-rights-heroes-video/.

CHAPTER 6: RAPE CULTURE FEMINISM

1. Seth Ferranti, "Why Are So Many Sex Offenders Getting Murdered in California's Prisons?" *Vice* magazine, February 18, 2015, http://www.vice.com/read/why-sex-offenders-are-getting-slaughtered-in-california-prisons-218.

2. Tara Culp-Ressler, "Study Finds 'Epidemic Level' of Rape on College Campus," *ThinkProgress* (blog), May 20, 2015, https://thinkprogress.org/study-finds-epidemic-level-of-rape-on-college-campus-52e93dcbbcf9.

3. Lauren Oyler, "Undeniably Massive Study Confirms Campus Rape Is an Undeniable, Massive Problem," Broadly, September 21, 2015, https://broadly.vice.com/en_us/article/new-study-validates-controversial-1-in-5-campus-sexual-assault-statistic.

4. "U.S. Bureau of Justice Statistics' Campus Climate Study Confirms Epidemic of College Sexual Assault," EROC (End Rape on Campus) website, January 27, 2016, http://endrapeoncampus.org/eroc-blog/2016/1/26/bjs-campus-climate-survey-key-highlights.

5. Sara Stewart, "How 'The Hunting Ground' Uncovers the Campus Rape Epidemic," *New York Post*, February 27, 2015, http://nypost.com/2015/02/27/how-the-hunting-ground-uncovers-the-campus-rape-epidemic/.

6. Emilie Buchwald, Pamela R. Fletcher, and Martha Roth, *Transforming a Rape Culture* (Minneapolis: Milkweed Editions, 1993).

7. "What Is Rape Culture?" the website WAVAW Rape Crisis Centre, accessed September 07, 2016, http://www.wavaw.ca/what-is-rape-culture/.

8. Suzannah Weiss, "4 College Traditions That Perpetuate Rape Culture," *Bustle*, May 9, 2016, http://www.bustle.com/articles/159661-4-college-traditions-that-perpetuate-rape-culture.

9. Paula Lavigne, "OTL: Women Say Baylor Ignored Sexual Assaults," ESPN, February 2, 2016, http://www.espn.com/espn/otl/story/_/id/14675790/baylor-officials-accused-failing-investigate-sexual-assaults-fully-adequately-providing-support-alleged-victims.

10. Christopher P. Krebs et al., *The Campus Sexual Assault (CSA) Study* (Report no. 221153) (Washington, D.C.: National Criminal Justice Reference Service, 2007).

11. Nick Anderson and Scott Clement, "Poll Shows That 20 Percent of Women Are Sexually Assaulted in College," *Washington Post*, June 12, 2015, http://www.washingtonpost.com/sf/local/2015/06/12/1-in-5-women-say-they-were-violated/.

12. Blake Neff, "Are 20 Percent of Women Really Assaulted in College?" *Daily Caller*, June 13, 2015, http://dailycaller.com/2015/06/13/are-20-percent-of-women-really-assaulted-in-college/.

13. Ashe Schow, "No, 1 in 5 Women Have Not Been Raped on College Campuses," *Washington Examiner*, August 13, 2014, http://www.washingtonexaminer.com/no-1-in-5-women-have-not-been-raped-on-college-campuses/article/2551980.

14. David Cantor et al., *Report on the AAU Campus Climate Survey on Sexual Assault and Sexual Misconduct* (Rockville, MD: Westat, September 21, 2015), http://www.aau.edu/uploadedFiles/AAU_Publications/AAU_Reports/Sexual_Assault_Campus_Survey/Report on the AAU Campus Climate Survey on Sexual Assault and Sexual Misconduct.pdf.

15. "Top Three Lies of Feminism | Milo Yiannopoulos," YouTube video, 8:37, in which Yiannopoulous takes on radical feminism, posted by Matthew Drake, January 24, 2016, https://www.youtube.com/watch?v=6FlEiW1qjeo.

16. Linda M. Lefauve, "Campus Rape Expert Can't Answer Basic Questions about His Sources," *Reason*, July 28, 2015, http://reason.com/archives/2015/07/28/campus-rape-statistics-lisak-problem.

17. Robby Soave, "How an Influential Campus Rape Study Skewed the Debate," *Hit & Run* (blog), July 28, 2015, http://reason.com/blog/2015/07/28/campus-rape-stats-lisak-study-wrong.

18. Sofi Sinozich and Lynn Langton, *Rape and Sexual Assault Victimization among College Age Females, 1995–2013* (Special Report), U.S. Department of Justice, December 2014, http://www.bjs.gov/content/pub/pdf/rsavcaf9513.pdf.

19. The *Federalist* Staff, "New DOJ Data on Sexual Assaults: Students Are Less Likely to Be Raped," *Federalist*, December 11, 2014, http://thefederalist.com/2014/12/11/new-doj-data-on-sexual-assaults-college-students-are-actually-less-likely-to-be-victimized/.

20. Nick Anderson, "These Colleges Have the Most Reports of Rape," *Washington Post*, June 7, 2016, https://www.washingtonpost.com/news/grade-point/wp/2016/06/07/these-colleges-have-the-most-reports-of-rape/.

21. "Facts about Reed: Detailed Enrollment," Reed College website, accessed September 7, 2016, https://www.reed.edu/ir/enrollment_more.html.

22. "The Hunting Ground," Rotten Tomatoes, accessed September 7, 2016, https://www.rottentomatoes.com/m/the_hunting_ground_2015/.

23. Emily Yoffe, "How *The Hunting Ground* Blurs the Truth," *Slate*, January 26, 2015, http://www.slate.com/articles/news_and_politics/doublex/2015/06/the_hunting_ground_a_closer_look_at_the_influential_documentary_reveals.html.

24. Ashe Schow, "'The Hunting Ground' Crew Caught Editing Wikipedia to Make Facts Conform to Film," *Washington Examiner*, November 19, 2015, http://www.washingtonexaminer.com/the-hunting-ground-crew-caught-editing-wikipedia-to-make-facts-conform-to-film/article/2576792.

25. Ashe Schow, "The Continuing Collapse of 'The Hunting Ground,' a Campus Sexual Assault Propaganda Film," *Washington Examiner*, June 3, 2015, http://www.washingtonexaminer.com/the-continuing-collapse-of-the-hunting-ground-a-campus-sexual-assault-propaganda-film/article/2565464.

26. Ashley Fantz, "Outrage over Six-Month Sentence in Stanford Rape Case," CNN, June 7, 2016, http://www.cnn.com/2016/06/06/us/sexual-assault-brock-turner-stanford/.

27. Blake Neff, "Columbia Mattress Girl to Attend State of the Union," *Daily Caller*, January 19, 2015, http://dailycaller.com/2015/01/19/columbia-mattress-girl-to-attend-state-of-the-union/.

28. Blake Neff, "The Text Of The Mattress Girl Lawsuit Will Shock You," *Daily Caller*, April 24, 2015, http://dailycaller.com/2015/04/24/the-text-of-the-mattress-girl-lawsuit-will-shock-you/.

29. Mike DeBonis and T. Rees Shapiro, "U-Va. President Suspends Fraternities until Jan. 9 in Wake of Rape Allegations," *Washington Post*, November 22, 2014, https://www.washingtonpost.com/local/education/u-va-president-suspends-fraternities-until-jan-9-in-wake-of-rape-allegations/2014/11/22/023d3688-7272-11e4-8808-afaa1e3a33ef_story.html.

30. Sheila Coronel, Steve Coll, and Derek Kravitz, "Rolling Stone and UVA: The Columbia University Graduate School of Journalism Report," *Rolling Stone*, April 5, 2015, http://www.rollingstone.com/culture/features/a-rape-on-campus-what-went-wrong-20150405.

31. Office of the Assistant Secretary for Civil Rights, "Dear Colleague Letter," U.S. Department of Education, April 4, 2011, http://www2.ed.gov/about/offices/list/ocr/letters/colleague-201104.html.

32. Will Creeley, "Why The Office for Civil Rights' April 'Dear Colleague Letter' Was 2011's Biggest FIRE Fight," FIRE, January 3, 2012, https://www.thefire.org/why-the-office-for-civil-rights-april-dear-colleague-letter-was-2011s-biggest-fire-fight/.

33. Ibid.

34. Blake Neff, "Michigan Admits It Screwed Up by Suspending Student for Rape," *Daily Caller*, September 16, 2015, http://dailycaller.com/2015/09/16/michigan-admits-it-screwed-up-by-suspending-student-for-rape/.

35. "Victory for Due Process: Student Punished for Alleged Sexual Assault Cleared by the University of North Dakota; Accuser Still Wanted for Lying to Police," FIRE, October 18, 2011, https://www.thefire.org/victory-for-due-process-student-punished-for-alleged-sexual-assault-cleared-by-university-of-north-dakota-accuser-still-wanted-for-lying-to-police-2/.

36. Jessica Luther, "The Wrestler and the Rape Victim," Vice Sports, December 15, 2014, https://sports.vice.com/en_us/article/the-wrestler-and-the-rape-victim.

37. Blake Neff, "Another Major College Rape Case Has Collapsed," *Daily Caller*, August 10, 2015, http://dailycaller.com/2015/08/10/another-major-college-rape-case-has-collapsed/.

38. Ezra Klein, "'Yes Means Yes' Is a Terrible Law, and I Completely Support It," *Vox*, October 13, 2014, http://www.vox.com/2014/10/13/6966847/yes-means-yes-is-a-terrible-bill-and-i-completely-support-it.

39. Emily Shire, "Is UMass-Amherst Biased against Male Students in Title IX Assault Cases?" *Daily Beast*, August 18, 2014, http://www.thedailybeast.com/articles/2014/08/18/is-umass-amherst-biased-against-male-students-in-title-ix-assault-cases.html.

40. Jessica Valenti, "Real Equality Is When Women Have the Right to Be as Drunk and Stupid as Men," *Guardian*, October 24, 2014, https://www.theguardian.com/commentisfree/2014/oct/24/real-equality-is-when-women-have-the-right-to-be-as-drunk-and-stupid-as-men.

41. Olga Khazan, "The Pros and Cons of Sorority Parties," *Atlantic*, January 21, 2015, http://www.theatlantic.com/education/archive/2015/01/the-pros-and-cons-of-sorority-parties/384670/.

42. Jen Yamato, "Why Don't Sororities Have the Right to Party Like Frats," *Daily Beast*, October 16, 2015, http://www.thedailybeast.com/articles/2016/05/14/why-don-t-sororities-have-the-right-to-party-like-frats.html.

43. Emily Yoffe, "The Best Rape Prevention: Tell College Women to Stop Getting So Wasted," *Slate*, October 15, 2013, http://www.slate.com/articles/double_x/doublex/2013/10/sexual_assault_and_drinking_teach_women_the_connection.html.

44. Kate McDonough, "Sorry, Emily Yoffe: Blaming Assault on Women's Drinking Is Wrong, Dangerous and Tired," *Salon*, October 16, 2013, http://www.salon.com/2013/10/16/blaming_assault_on_womens_drinking_is_tired_dangerous_rape_apology/.

45. Hanna Rosin, "Boys on the Side," *Atlantic*, September, 2012, http://www.theatlantic.com/magazine/archive/2012/09/boys-on-the-side/309062/.

46. Justin Garcia et al., "Sexual Hook-Up Culture," American Psychological Association, February 2013, http://www.apa.org/monitor/2013/02/ce-corner.aspx.

47. "Study on College Hook-Ups," ABC News, July 26, 2016, http://abcnews.go.com/GMA/story?id=126813&page=1.

48. Leah Fessler, "Modern Love," *Middlebury Magazine*, July 27, 2015, http://sites.middlebury.edu/middmag/2015/07/27/modern-love/.

49. John Birger, "Unequal Gender Ratios at Colleges Are Driving Hookup Culture," *Time*, October 15, 2015, http://time.com/money/4072951/college-gender-ratios-dating-hookup-culture/.

CHAPTER 7: GREEKS UNDER SIEGE

1. Caitlin Flanagan, "The Dark Power of Fraternities," *Atlantic*, March 2014, http://www.theatlantic.com/magazine/archive/2014/03/the-dark-power-of-fraternities/357580/.

2. Walter M. Kimbrough, "The Hazing Problem at Black Fraternities," *Atlantic*, March 17, 2014, http://www.theatlantic.com/education/archive/2014/03/the-hazing-problem-at-black-fraternities/284452/.

3. "New Fraternity Picks Senator Goldwater as Grand Wizard," *Harvard Crimson*, November 30, 1960, http://www.thecrimson.com/article/1960/11/30/new-fraternity-picks-senator-goldwater-as/.

4. "Constantine, Heraldry and Roman Heritage," Sigma Chi Fraternity, accessed September 9, 2016, http://sigmachi.org/constantine-heraldry-and-roman-heritage.

5. Jay Reeves, "Kappa Alpha Fraternity, Inspired by Robert E. Lee, Bans Confederate Rebel Uniforms," *AL.com* (blog), April 22, 2010, http://blog.al.com/spotnews/2010/04/kappa_alpha_fraternity_inspire.html.

6. See *Oracle: The Research Journal of the Association of Fraternity Advisors* 2, no. 1 (February 2006), http://c.ymcdn.com/sites/www.afa1976.org/resource/collection/0E038C73-3450-45DA-A3B4-C5C64D5ED39B/V2_Iss1_Oracle_Feb_2006.pdf; Peter Jacobs, "People Who Were in Frats and Sororities Are Better at Their Jobs," *Business Insider*, May 28, 2014, http://www.businessinsider.com/hire-fraternity-sorority-member-2014-5.

7. See "NAACP v. Patterson 357 U.S. 449 (1958)," Justia Law, 2016, accessed September 9, 2016, https://supreme.justia.com/cases/federal/us/357/449/case.html.

8. Matthew W Hughey, "A Paradox of Participation: Nonwhites in White Sororities and Fraternities," *Social Problems* 57, no. 4 (2010): 655–56.

9. "Fraternities & Sororities," Princeton University, last updated May 6, 2011, https://www.princeton.edu/reports/2011/campuslife/obs-rec/fraternities-sororities/.

10. Hughey, "A Paradox of Participation," 658.

11. Abbey Crain and Matt Ford, "The Final Barrier: 50 Years Later, Segregation Still Exists," *Crimson White*, September 11, 2013, http://www.cw.ua.edu/article/2013/09/the-final-barrier-50-years-later-segregation-still-exists.

12. Stephen Dethrage, "Jesse Jackson Speaks on Segregation in University of Alabama Greek System, Suggests Picketing Sorority Houses," *AL.com*, September 14, 2013, http://blog.al.com/tuscaloosa/2013/09/jesse_jackson_weighs_in_on_seg.html.

13. Victor Luckerson, "University of Alabama Moves to End Segregated Sorority System," *Time*, September 16, 2013, http://nation.time.com/2013/09/16/university-of-alabama-moves-to-end-segregated-sorority-system/.

14. See "Racist Sororities at the University of Alabama," YouTube video, 9:39, posted by *Vice*, October 23, 2013, https://www.youtube.com/watch?v=on0mT8MQ-Wg.

15. Tyler Kingkade, "University of Alabama Student Government Finally Votes for Integrating Greek System," *Huffington Post*, April 21, 2014, http://www.huffingtonpost.com/2014/04/21/university-of-alabama-greek-integrate_n_5187263.html?utm_hp_ref=black-voices.

16. A. L. Bailey, "'Bama Sorority Video Worse for Women than Donald Trump," *AL.com*, August 14, 2015, http://www.al.com/opinion/index.ssf/2015/08/bama_sorority_video_worse_for.html.

17. Kristen Rein, "U. of Alabama Sorority Criticized for Recruitment Video," *USA Today*, August 18, 2015, http://www.usatoday.com/story/news/nation-now/2015/08/18/university-alabama-criticized-racially-homogeneous-recruitment-video/31900097/.

18. Tyler Kingkade, "Emails Show How Quickly the Oklahoma SAE Scandal Unfolded," *Huffington Post*, May 29, 2015, http://www.huffingtonpost.com/2015/05/29/emails-oklahoma-sae-scandal_n_7470972.html.

19. Eugene Volokh, "No, It's Not Constitutional for the University of Oklahoma to Expel Students for Racist Speech [UPDATED in Light of the Students' Expulsion]," *Washington Post*, March 10, 2015, http://www.washingtonpost.com/news/volokh-conspiracy/wp/2015/03/10/no-a-public-university-may-not-expel-students-for-racist-speech/.

20. Eugene Volokh, "What Speech Is Going to Justify Expulsion Next, If the OU / SAE Expulsion Is Accepted as Proper?" *Washington Post*, March 10, 2015, https://www.washingtonpost.com/news/volokh-conspiracy/wp/2015/03/10/what-speech-is-going-to-justify-expulsion-next/?utm_term=.959f13f7c552.

21. Associated Press, "Timeline: List of Recent Sorority and Fraternity Racist Incidents," *USA Today*, March 15, 2015, http://college.usatoday.com/2015/03/15/timeline-list-of-recent-sorority-and-fraternity-racist-incidents/.

22. David J.Herzig and Samuel D. Brunson, "Subsidized Injustice," *Slate,* March 13, 2015, http://www.slate.com/articles/news_and_politics/jurisprudence/2015/03/racist_fraternities_sororities_and_universities_should_have_their_tax_exempt.html.

23. Jessica Bennett, "Campus Sexual Assault: The Problem with Frats Isn't Just Rape. It's Power" *Time*, December 3, 2014, http://time.com/3616158/fraternity-rape-uva-rolling-stone-sexual-assault/.

24. Colin Downes, "Greek Gangs," *Slate,* December 5, 2014, http://www.slate.com/articles/news_and_politics/jurisprudence/2014/12/fraternity_sexual_assault_and_criminal_activities_states_should_use_gang.html.

25. Chuck Ross, "UVA President Admits Rolling Stone Gang Rape Article Is 'Discredited,'" *Daily Caller*, January 1, 2015, http://dailycaller.com/2015/01/30/uva-president-admits-rolling-stone-gang-rape-article-is-discredited/#ixzz4K3afTQfZ.

26. "Nationwide: 'All-Comers' Policies Jeopardize Free Association," Foundation for Individual Rights in Education, accessed September 12, 2016, https://www.thefire.org/cases/nationwide-all-comers-policies-jeopardize-free-association/.

27. Leah Finnegan, "Former Vanderbilt Fraternity Members Allege Unfair Treatment Based on Sexuality," *Huffington Post*, May 1, 2011, http://www.huffingtonpost.com/2010/11/05/vanderbilt-beta-upsilon-chi_n_779485.html.

28. Pierce Greenberg and Jerome Botcher, "At Vanderbilt, All-Comers Policy and Athletics Butt Heads," Nashville *City Paper*, May 20, 2012, http://nashvillecitypaper.com/content/city-news/vanderbilt-all-comers-policy-and-athletics-butt-heads.

29. "Vanderbilt 'All-Comers' Policy and Its Implications for Greek Organizations," *Fraternal Law*, March 2012.

30. Scott Greer, "The Frat Site That Helped Ignite #TheChalkening Speaks Out," *Daily Caller*, April 4, 2016, http://dailycaller.com/2016/04/04/the-frat-site-that-helped-ignite-thechalkening-speaks-out/.

CHAPTER 8: ART OF THE HOAX

1. Shapiro, T. Rees. "Lawyers in Rolling Stone Lawsuit File New Evidence That 'Jackie' Created Fake Persona." *Washington Post.* May 18, 2016. Accessed September 06, 2016.

2. Sasha Goldstein. "Crystal Mangum, Duke Lacrosse Accuser, Convicted in Boyfriend's Stabbing Death," *New York Daily News,* November 22, 2013, http://www.nydailynews.com/news/crime/crystal-mangum-duke-lacrosse-accuser-convicted-boyfriend-stabbing-death-article-1.1526467; Oren Dorell, "Nifong Wins Election to Remain as D.A. in Durham, N.C.," *USA Today,* May 3, 2006, http://usatoday30.usatoday.com/sports/college/lacrosse/2006-05-02-durham-election_x.htm.

3. Miller, Michael E. "Yale Investigation Finds 'no Evidence' of Racism at Frat Party Alleged to Have Been for 'White Girls Only'." *Washington Post.* December 11, 2015. Accessed September 06, 2016. https://www.washingtonpost.com/news/morning-mix/wp/2015/12/11/yale-investigation-finds-no-evidence-of-racism-at-frat-party-alleged-to-have-been-for-white-girls-only/.

4. Scott Greer, "Was Mizzou's President Forced out over Wildly Exaggerated Claims?" *Daily Caller,* November 12, 2015, http://dailycaller.com/2015/11/12/was-mizzous-president-forced-out-over-wildly-exaggerated-claims/.

5. Blake Neff, "Mizzou Students Hallucinate KKK On Campus," *Daily Caller,* November 11, 2015, http://dailycaller.com/2015/11/11/mizzou-students-hallucinate-kkk-on-campus/.

6. Scott Greer, "Far More People Claim Alien Abduction Than KKK Membership," *Daily Caller,* March 1, 2016, http://dailycaller.com/2016/03/01/far-more-people-claim-alien-abduction-than-membership-in-the-kkk/.

7. Chuck Ross, "Meet the Privileged Obama-Supporting White Kids Who Perpetrated Cruel Oberlin Race Hoax," *Daily Caller,* August 22, 2013, http://dailycaller.com/2013/08/22/meet-the-privileged-obama-supporting-white-kids-who-perpetrated-cruel-oberlin-race-hoax/.

8. Blake Neff, "SUNY-Albany Student Finally Confesses to Hillary-Fooling Hate Crime HOAX," *Daily Caller,* June 22, 2016, http://dailycaller.com/2016/06/22/suny-albany-student-finally-confesses-to-hillary-fooling-hate-crime-hoax/.

9. Blake Neff, "Black Iowa Student Starts Fight, Loses, Makes Up Hate Crime, Gets Caught," *Daily Caller,* May 17, 2016, http://dailycaller.com/2016/05/17/black-iowa-student-starts-fight-loses-makes-up-hate-crime-gets-caught/.

10. Eric Owens, "Surprise! Campus Noose Drawing Was Created by Black Students. NO CHARGES FILED For 'Hate Crime'," *Daily Caller,* April 28, 2016, http://dailycaller.com/2016/04/28/campus-noose-drawing-was-created-by-black-students/.

11. Eric Owens, "Guy Who Threatened to 'Shoot Every Black' Kid on Campus . . . Is Black," *Daily Caller,* November 20, 2015, http://dailycaller.com/2015/11/20/guy-who-threatened-to-shoot-every-black-kid-on-campus-is-black/.

12. Eric Owens, "JUSTICE: Judge Sends Black Activist to Jail for Hoax Death Threats to Black Students, Faculty," *Daily Caller*, June 19, 2016, http://dailycaller.com/2016/06/19/justice-judge-sends-black-activist-to-jail-for-hoax-death-threats-to-black-students-faculty/.

13. Gabriela Julia and Marlee Tuskes, "UB Art Student Admits to Hanging 'White Only' and 'Black Only' Signs on Campus," *Spectrum*. September 16, 2015, http://www.ubspectrum.com/article/2015/09/ub-student-admits-to-hanging-white-only-and-black-only-signs-for-art-project.

14. Owens, Eric. "Wyoming 'Hate-F***' Hoaxer Adds to Checkered Criminal Past, Now Attends Law School," *Daily Caller*, October 12, 2013, http://dailycaller.com/2013/10/12/wyoming-hate-f-hoaxer-adds-to-checkered-criminal-past-now-attends-law-school/.

15. Regina Garcia Cano, "Gay Man Says North Dakota Frat Choked, Beat and Stripped Him," *Huffington Post,* September 4, 2015, http://www.huffingtonpost.com/entry/north-dakota-frat_us_55e97840e4b002d5c075aa96.

16. Eric Owens, "SURPRISE! Another 'Anti-Gay' Hate Crime Turns Out to Be a Big Hoax," *Daily Caller*, October 13, 2015, http://dailycaller.com/2015/10/13/another-anti-gay-hate-crime-turns-out-to-be-a-big-hoax/.

17. Eric Owens, "Lesbian Professor Punched Herself, Swore Random Guy Beat Her," *The Daily Caller.* March 11, 2016. Accessed September 06, 2016, http://dailycaller.com/2016/03/11/lesbian-professor-cold-cocked-her-own-face-then-swore-random-guy-beat-her-up-at-toby-keith-concert/.

18. Blake Neff, "Students Double Down, Insist Fake Hate Crime Was Real," *Daily Caller*, September 25, 2015, http://dailycaller.com/2015/09/25/students-double-down-insist-fake-hate-crime-was-real/.

CHAPTER 9: WHITHER WILL CAMPUS INSANITY TAKE AMERICA?

1. Dennis Prager, "Conservative Parents, Left-Wing Children," *National Review*, November 5, 2013, http://www.nationalreview.com/article/363082/conservative-parents-left-wing-children-dennis-prager.

2. Heather Saul, "Lena Dunham Forced off Twitter by Misogynistic Trolls," *Independent*, September 30, 2015, http://www.independent.co.uk/news/people/lena-dunham-forced-off-twitter-after-abusive-trolls-who-turned-it-into-an-unsafe-space-a6673581.html.

3. Robert Chilman, "Microaggression: The Next HR Nightmare? (Or Why You Should Listen to Your Mother)," *Linked In* (blog), December 3, 2015, https://www.linkedin.com/pulse/microaggression-next-hr-nightmare-why-you-should-listen-chilman.

4. Tom Leonard, "Queen of Cynicism: No Stunt's Too Shameless for Beyonce, Who Was Once Accused of Trying to Look White but This Week Posed as a Heroine of Black Power," *Daily Mail*, February 12, 2016, http://www.dailymail.co.uk/news/article-3445116/Queen-cynicism-No-stunt-s-shameless-Beyonce-accused-trying-look-white-week-posed-heroine-black-power.html.

5. Ebenezer Samuel, "Foster Leads 4 Dolphins in Protest, Chiefs' Peters Raises Fist," *New York Daily News*, September 12, 2016, http://www.nydailynews.com/sports/football/chiefs-cb-marcus-peters-black-power-salute-anthem-article-1.2787509.

6. See Robert D. Putnam, *Bowling Alone: The Collapse and Revival of American Community* (New York: Simon & Schuster, 2000).

7. Ta-Nehisi Coates, "Hillary Clinton Was Politically Incorrect, but She Wasn't Wrong About Trump's Supporters," *Atlantic*, September 10, 2016, http://www.theatlantic.com/politics/archive/2016/09/basket-of-deplorables/499493/.

8. Eric Owens, "Ohio State Ends Student Occupation with Promise of Expulsion," *Daily Caller*, April 9, 2016, http://dailycaller.com/2016/04/09/ohio-state-swiftly-ends-students-occupation-with-promises-of-arrest-expulsion-video/.

9. Julia Glum, "ITT Tech Shutdown: Loan Forgiveness for Students Possible as For-Profit College Chain Closes," *International Business Times*, September 6, 2016, http://www.ibtimes.com/itt-tech-shutdown-loan-forgiveness-students-possible-profit-college-chain-closes-2411834.

10. Michael Stratford, "Federal Scrutiny of Campus Sexual Assaults Spills into the States," *Inside Higher Ed*, August 28, 2014, https://www.insidehighered.com/news/2014/08/28/federal-scrutiny-campus-sexual-assaults-spills-states.

11. Katherine Weber, "Tenn. Governor Vetoes Vanderbilt Bill; All-Comers Policy to Remain in Place," *CP* Middle East, May 3, 2012, http://www.christianpost.com/news/tenn-governor-vetoes-vanderbilt-bill-all-comers-policy-to-remain-in-place-74331/.

12. Scott Greer, "Tennessee Legislators Look to Defund Campus Police for Political Correctness Rules," *Campus Reform*, March 7, 2013, http://campusreform.org/?ID=4650.

13. Scott Greer, "UPDATE: U of Tennessee to Cut State Funding for Controversial Sex Week," *Campus Reform*, March 22, 2013, http://campusreform.org/?ID=4677.

14. Scott Greer, "Tennessee Lawmakers Rip Apart University System for Spending Millions on 'Diversity Programming,'" *Daily Caller*, October 15, 2015, http://dailycaller.com/2015/10/15/tn-lawmakers-rip-apart-university-system-for-spending-millions-on-diversity-programming/.

15. Scott Greer, "The University of Tennessee Is Waging a Literal War on Christmas," *Daily Caller*, December 5, 2015, http://dailycaller.com/2015/12/05/the-university-of-tennessee-is-waging-a-literal-war-on-christmas/.

16. Richard Locker, "University of Tennessee Diversity Funding Bill Allowed to Become Law," *Tennessean*, May 20, 2016, http://www.tennessean.com/story/news/politics/2016/05/20/university-tennessee-diversity-funding-bill-allowed-become-law/84650208/.

17. Jessica Chasmar, "University of Missouri Sees 25% Enrollment Drop, $32M Budget Deficit after Racial Protests," *Washington Times*, March 10, 2016, http://www.washingtontimes.com/news/2016/mar/10/university-of-missouri-sees-25-enrollment-drop-32m/.

18. Blake Neff, "Mizzou Closing Four Whole Dorms Because of Collapsing Enrollment," *Daily Caller*, April 12, 2016, http://dailycaller.com/2016/04/12/mizzou-closing-four-whole-dorms-because-of-collapsing-enrollment/.

19. Rudi Keller, "University of Missouri Fundraising Takes $6 Million Hit in December as Donors Hold Back Funds," *Columbia Daily Tribune*, February 21, 2016, http://www.columbiatribune.com/news/education/turmoil_at_mu/university-of-missouri-fundraising-takes-million-hit-in-december-as/article_ed7cfd5b-3b3e-5b18-95d9-f2945ac51172.html.

20. "Spotlight," FIRE, accessed September 19, 2016, https://www.thefire.org/spotlight/.

21. David O. Sacks and Peter A. Thiel, *The Diversity Myth: "Multiculturalism" and the Politics of Intolerance at Stanford* (Oakland, CA: Independent Institute, 1995).

EPIL●GUE: TRUMP'S WIN'S AND CAMPUS INSANITY

1. Eric Owens, "The Daily Caller's YUGE Roundup Of Campus Freakouts After Trump's Victory." *Daily Caller*, November 10, 2016, http://dailycaller.com/2016/11/10/no-safe-space-the-daily-callers-yuge-roundup-of-campus-freakouts-after-trumps-victory-video/.

2. Rebecca Flood, "Schools across America offer counselling in the wake of Trump's shock presidential win," *The Express*, November 10, 2016, http://www.express.co.uk/news/world/730910/Donald-Trump-school-counselling-America-election-Clinton-vote-students.

3. Annabel Scott, "College Students Now Demanding 'Sanctuary Campuses' To Protect Illegals From Trump," *Daily Caller*, November 15, 2016, http://dailycaller.com/2016/11/15/college-students-now-demanding-sanctuary-campuses-to-protect-illegals-from-trump/.

4. Elaine Korry, "The Return of the Students for a Democratic Society," *NPR*. January 30, 2006, http://www.npr.org/templates/story/story.php?storyId=5178648.

5. Cathy Renna, "A Vote for Trump Was A Hate Crime," *Huffington Post*, November 10, 2016, http://www.huffingtonpost.com/entry/a-vote-for-trump-was-a-hate-crime_us_58249871e4b0edfa1393613a.

6. Christian Datoc, "Trump Apologizes After Hidden Cam Video Surfaces Of Him Talking Lewd About Women," *Daily Caller*, October 7, 2016, http://dailycaller.com/2016/10/07/trump-apologizes-after-hidden-cam-video-surfaces-of-him-talking-lewd-about-women-video/

7. Marina Koren, "Donald Trump's No-Apology Tour Continues," *The Atlantic*. August 25, 2015, http://www.theatlantic.com/politics/archive/2015/08/donald-trump-is-not-sorry/402295/.

8. Pam Key, "Trump: Political Correctness Is Killing Us, We Have to Look At Profiling," *Breitbart News*, June 19, 2016, http://www.breitbart.com/video/2016/06/19/trump-political-correctness-is-killing-us-we-have-to-look-at-profiling/.

9. Scott Greer, "For Democrats, Identity Politics Trump Economic Populism," *Daily Caller*, May 25, 2016, http://dailycaller.com/2016/05/25/for-democrats-identity-politics-trumps-economic-populism/.

10. Blake Neff, "Donald Trump Says Mizzou Protesters Are 'Disgusting,' 'Crazy'," *Daily Caller*, November 12, 2015, http://dailycaller.com/2015/11/12/donald-trump-says-mizzou-protesters-are-disgusting-crazy-video/.

11. Sean Trende and David Byler, "Republican Party the Strongest It's Been In 80 Years," *RealClearPolitics*, November 17, 2016, http://www.realclearpolitics.com/articles/2016/11/17/republican_party_the_strongest_its_been_in_80_years.html.

APPENDIX: THE GREAT COLLEGE SWINDLE

1. Jillian Berman, "America's Growing Student-Loan-Debt Crisis," *MarketWatch*, January 19, 2016, http://www.marketwatch.com/story/americas-growing-student-loan-debt-crisis-2016-01-15.

2. Emily Peck, "The Class of 2015 Is in for a Rude Awakening on Pay," *Huffington Post*, May 12, 2015, http://www.huffingtonpost.com/2015/05/12/college-grad-starting-salary_n_7265090.html.

3. Leah McGrath Goodman, "Millennial College Graduates: Young, Educated, Jobless," *Newsweek*, May 27, 2016, http://www.newsweek.com/2015/06/05/millennial-college-graduates-young-educated-jobless-335821.html.

4. Alyssa Davis, Will Kimball, and Gould Elise, "The Class of 2015: Despite an Improving Economy, Young Grads Still Face an Uphill Climb," Economic Policy Institute, May 27, 2015, http://www.epi.org/publication/the-class-of-2015/.

5. Stephen Dash, "Why Student Loans Are So Difficult to Discharge in Bankruptcy," *Forbes*, October 25, 2015, http://www.forbes.com/sites/stephendash/2015/10/25/why-student-loans-are-so-difficult-to-discharge-in-bankruptcy/.

6. Ryan Gorman, "How Student-Loan Debt Is Dragging Down the Economy," *Business Insider*, May 1, 2015, http://www.businessinsider.com/3-charts-explain-the-effect-of-student-loans-on-the-economy-2015-5.

7. Andrew Josuweit, "Where the Candidates Stand on Student-loan Debt," CNBC, April 4, 2016, http://www.cnbc.com/2016/04/04/where-the-candidates-stand-on-student-loan-debt-commentary.html.

8. Tyler Kingkade, "New Analysis Shows Problematic Boom in Higher Ed Administrators," *Huffington Post*, February 6, 2014, http://www.huffingtonpost.com/2014/02/06/higher-ed-administrators-growth_n_4738584.html.

9. Benjamin Ginsberg, "Administrators Ate My Tuition," *Washington Monthly*, September 5, 2016, http://washingtonmonthly.com/magazine/septoct-2011/administrators-ate-my-tuition/.

10. Paul F. Campos, "The Real Reason College Tuition Costs So Much," *New York Times*, April 4, 2015, http://www.nytimes.com/2015/04/05/opinion/sunday/the-real-reason-college-tuition-costs-so-much.html?_r=0.

11: Erik Brady, Jodi Upton, and Steve Berkowitz, "Can College Athletics Continue to Spend Like This?" *USA Today*, April 23, 2016, http://www.usatoday.com/story/sports/college/2016/04/17/ncaa-football-basketball-power-five-revenue-expenses/83035862/.

12. Sara Ganim and Devin Sayers, "UNC Athletics Report Finds 18 Years of Academic Fraud," CNN, October 23, 2014, http://www.cnn.com/2014/10/22/us/unc-report-academic-fraud/.

13. Sara Ganim, "Some College Athletes Play Like Adults, Read Like Fifth-Graders," CNN, May 25, 2014, http://www.cnn.com/interactive/2014/01/us/college-scores/index.html.

14. Jake New, "More Than a Dozen Athletic Programs Have Committed Academic Fraud in Last Decade, with More Likely to Come," *Inside Higher Ed,* July 8, 2016, https://www.insidehighered.com/news/2016/07/08/more-dozen-athletic-programs-have-committed-academic-fraud-last-decade-more-likely.

15. Paula Lavigne, "Baylor Faces Accusations of Ignoring Sex Assault Victims," ESPN, February 2, 2016, http://www.espn.com/espn/otl/story/_/id/14675790/baylor-officials-accused-failing-investigate-sexual-assaults-fully-adequately-providing-support-alleged-victims.

16. Associated Press, "3 More Women Sue Baylor over Reaction to Rape Allegations," *LA Times*, June 15, 2016, http://www.latimes.com/nation/nationnow/la-na-baylor-rape-lawsuit-20160615-snap-story.html.

17. Nate Rau and Anita Wadhwani, "Tennessee Settles Sexual Assault Suit for $2.48 Million," *Tennessean*, July 6, 2016, http://www.tennessean.com/story/news/crime/2016/07/05/tennessee-settles-sexual-assault-suit-248-million/86708442/.

18. Dustin Dopirak, "Lawsuit: UT Football Players Assaulted Drae Bowles for Helping Rape Victim," *Knoxville News Sentinel*, February 11, 2016, http://www.knoxnews.com/sports/vols/football/lawsuit-ut-football-players-assaulted-drae-bowles-for-helping-rape-victim-2b605b1c-9e5f-56e5-e053-01-368262521.html.

19. Blake Neff, "Oklahoma: Tough on Racism, Weak on Assault, Burglary," *Daily Caller*, March 11, 2015, http://dailycaller.com/2015/03/11/oklahoma-tough-on-racism-weak-on-assault-burglary/; Paula Lavigne, "Missouri Has Second-Highest Number of Alleged in Sex Assaults in OTL Study," ESPN, July 13, 2015, http://www.espn.com/blog/ncfnation/post/_/id/111520/otl-missouri-had-second-highest-number-of-athletes-alleged-in-sex-assaults.

20. Jeffrey J. Selingo, "Why Are So Many College Students Failing to Gain Job Skills before Graduation?" *Washington Post*, January 26, 2015, https://www.washingtonpost.com/news/grade-point/wp/2015/01/26/why-are-so-many-college-students-failing-to-gain-job-skills-before-graduation/.

21. Kelley Holland, "Why Johnny Can't Write, and Why Employers Are Mad," CNBC, November 11, 2013, http://www.cnbc.com/2013/11/08/why-johnny-cant-write-and-why-employers-are-mad.html.

INDEX

THE **TRUTH** OF **FERGUSON**

THE WAR ON POLICE tells what really happened on the front lines and behind the scenes during the mayhem and upheaval of Ferguson and then follows the trail to explain what is happening across the country. The country is at a boiling point, and it's time to know the truth.

RACIAL VIOLENCE is BACK!

In this latest edition of 'WHITE GIRL BLEED A LOT', award-winning reporter Colin Flaherty breaks the code of silence on the explosion of racial violence in more than one-hundred cities since 2010 and makes an undeniable case for one of the largest and most underreported problems facing America today.

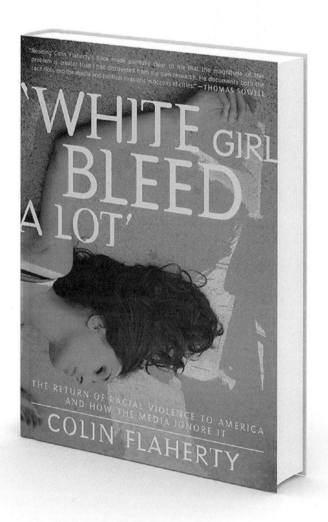